LIVING IN A TIME OF DYING

CRIES OF GRIEF, RAGE, LOVE, AND HOPE

MEGHAN ELIZABETH TAUCK

WILLIAM DOUGLAS HORDEN

As Within Publishing

ISBN (paperback): 978-1-7377833-0-5
ISBN (ebook): 978-1-7377833-1-2

This book is dedicated to G,
and to all the young ones who will inherit the past
and dream the future into being.

If you want things to stay the same, everything will have to change.

~ Giuseppi Tomasi di Lampedusa
The Leopard

TABLE OF CONTENTS

Preface

We take up writing this book in the Fall of 2020, in the midst of the pandemic so affecting civilization at the moment.

The future reader can research this time to better grasp the strangeness of the situation people everywhere in the world experienced during this outbreak—and from the distance afforded by time, enjoy a perspective of certainty about how and when the pandemic passed; and what it left in its passing.

But here, in the throes of it all, humanity drifts in the uncertainty, still a fractured entity of political interests and corporate greed. This is complicated by the ongoing trials and vicissitudes of daily life in an era of environmental distress and social upheaval. Anxiety, denial, and frustration fill the daily lives of individuals living through this turbulence with no apparent end in sight.

Even the most objective eye at this time cannot discern the changes this disease will wring from the hearts and minds of human nature, nor can the most objective mind help but wonder what civilization might look like in its wake. The seriousness of this virus and its consequences are ultimately unpredictable at this juncture, making the uncertainty of the time a matter of profound impact as much on the collective unconscious as on the collective consciousness.

We articulate all this as clearly and simply as possible, in the hope of sharing the grief and rage and love and hope which we are all facing at this unique turning point in the history of humankind.

We are all born under a death sentence, of course, but we do not all live with the "ax over our heads" on a daily basis. Nor with the daily concern for the immediate safety and wellbeing of all we know and love.

It is difficult not to think back on the plague that struck Mexico in the early years of the Conquest, when half the population succumbed to a disease for which they had no immunity—how the people of that day must have suffered, enduring not only their own demise but that of their civilization as well.

How it must have appeared as though their gods had forsaken them.

How little the human psyche has changed since.

Meghan Elizabeth Tauck   William Douglas Horden
Ithaca, New York   Delicias, Chihuahua

INTRODUCTION

If I could utter a scream commensurate to the justice that Grief deserves, it would rend the world into dust, into infinite billions of fragmentary particles, each echoing the devastation of my heart. This is the experience of Grief felt by anyone who has lost something—or someone—that cannot be replaced. It is not mine alone. It is all of ours.

What does it mean that humanity is headed for extinction, or that everything and everyone we love and value in this world— whole species of birds, and with them their song; the sweet nectar of peaches and all the fruits dependent on the steadily waning colonies of bees; maple syrup boiled on a crisp snow-capped day in March; the chorus of peeping frogs heralding the release from winter's grasp; fireflies in June; the slow baptism of a summer rain instead of an intermittent deluge; the dependable assurance of the seasons—is potentially, if not inevitably, going to suffer and be irrevocably lost?

When I open my heart and let myself feel—*really feel*—the love and gratitude for this land that has borne me, literally birthed me, nourished and supported me, called itself my home, its creatures my kin, and I its child, in rushes the weight of a piercing, all-encompassing Grief, so big and powerful that it threatens to split me open in shock and disbelief.

The dying is palpable. Climate-change fueled wildfires consuming millions of acres across the globe; people being beaten and killed in the streets; the ongoing floods of refugees seeking sanctuary; disappeared and murdered Indigenous women throughout the Americas; the never-ending repression of entire populations by their more martial neighbors, or by their own governments. Meanwhile we hunker through a global pandemic that has shown what happens when countries juggle people's health with the health of economies: both options signal mass deaths—either from the spread of Covid-19 if we prioritize the economy, or from potential starvation and homelessness if we close down economies to prioritize people's health. It's a lose-lose situation, all part of the looming repercussions of two centuries of neoliberal capitalism.

Not to mention, of course, the much larger looming catastrophe—that of climate collapse and subsequent mass extinction.

It is overwhelming to consider the cascading litany of abuses and poor choices made by the world's superpowers *on behalf of literally all beings and all life on planet earth.* Choices that have led us to this impossible, irreconcilable moment of dying.

Humanity stands at a precipice, gazing into the abyss of our own twilight. We do not want to believe it—we deny it and prevaricate, insist that there is still something to be done, that some as yet undiscovered or simply under-funded technology will save us. Or, even accepting the impending collapse of not only human civilization but the global ecosystem in which we have evolved, that somehow some of us will survive and thrive again. And who knows? No one can tell the future. Maybe some will survive, for a time. But, when all is said and done, these are merely equivocations, fantasies we tell ourselves because we cannot (or will not) comprehend our own non-existence.

Do you remember the first time you entertained the inevitability of your own death? Do you recall the dizzying incomprehensibility of a world without you in it? Or, perhaps worse still, of a world, sometime in the future, without any of the people who have known and loved you, as they will all also inevitably pass away? Perhaps a world in which no trace of you—of your identity, your life, your existence—still remains? A world, in short, that does not remember you.

Such a world is literally inconceivable to us because, necessarily, the only world we *can* know is one with us in it. We know the world through the apparatus of our own existence. Hence a world without us might as well not exist. And yet we know, rationally, that it does. That it will.

This presents a profound cognitive dissonance. It is much easier to simply deny our eventual demise, at least until we are standing unavoidably face-to-face with it. In the meantime, we use our life's energy to make an impact, to leave something of ourselves behind for posterity: we breed, erect monuments, make lasting works of art, cement our legacies of wealth or influence to pass on in perpetuity, always with the stamp of our Name. Or else we resolve to simply survive and enjoy what passing fancies offer us pleasures in the interim.

There's nothing wrong with these endeavors in and of themselves. We all deserve pleasure and fulfillment in our lives. But insofar as they are engaged as a distraction from the full truth of the present moment, then they are at best a lost opportunity and at worst an active choice to perpetuate harm. Because the full truth of the present moment is that we are always, individually, standing face-to-face with our own demise, with death. Shit happens, bodies break and breakdown, and any of us could die at any moment. That is always true.

What is perhaps even more poignantly distressing, is that the full truth of *this* present moment is that we are *all* standing unavoidably face-to-face with the extinction of humanity through, if not nuclear or biological war, then the irrevocable, irreversible disruption of the global ecosystem that has supported our evolving biology since, literally, time immemorial. The full incomprehensible heart-rending truth of this moment is that humanity is standing at a precipice, staring into the abyss of its own—our own—extinction.

How does one live with that?

How do we live in a time of dying?

Some courageously attempt to stem the tide of the impending disaster that we ourselves have wrought upon the earth. They fight against the formidable tide of history, culture, entrenched power structures, and the emotional dysregulation of fear and greed. They struggle against the tsunami of that which cannot be stopped.

Some deny the present truth outright, preferring to believe in narratives that do not threaten the familiar, comfortable status quo. They uphold, perpetuate, and exacerbate the fear, greed, cultural mores, and systems of power and social control that have brought us to this harrowing precipice for the benefit of a very few at the expense of the vast many.

Some simply go about business as usual, either out of a complete loss for how to respond or simply because they are too overwhelmed by the enormity of what we are facing without any possibility of a ready panacea. They simply don't know what they can possibly do to alleviate the situation. Or, to appease their conscience, they do the bare minimum, whatever is within easy reach without having to upend the only way of life they've ever known.

Meanwhile, many—the vast majority of humans on this planet at this time (not to mention nonhumans)—continue to struggle just to survive with what meager resources have been allocated or left available to them. These impoverished, subjugated peoples—predominantly Black, Brown, and/or Indigenous people of color—drown, starve, expire from avoidable diseases, or are buried or burned alive in the wake of capitalism's colonialist greed (or colonialism's capitalist greed—which comes first, the chicken or the egg...) and the snow-balling breakdown of our global ecosystem and social structures.

Again, we ask: how do we live with this? How do we live with what we have done and continue to do?

There *is* another option—and increasingly the only one left to us as we creep closer and closer to that edge, to face the now unavoidable.

It is no different than sitting in the physician's office and being told one has a terminal disease.

We can, and must, recognize and accept the reality of our situation.

We can, and must, move this recognition and acceptance from the head into the heart.

We can, and must, *feel* it.

~

What follows is a spiritual manifesto for our times. It is our contribution to the collective effort to midwife this world into the next, and humanity in its evolution of consciousness.

Each chapter has been written on its own as an imperative expression of the authors' own processes of reckoning with

Grief, Rage, Love, and Hope in this Time of Dying. The chapters proceed in a back-and-forth between the two authors in a loose dialectic, and the reader will, no doubt, detect the distinctive voices of the authors, revealing their respective histories, influences, temperaments, and perspectives.

William Douglas Horden was born in a cemetery in Ohio in the year 1950. As a young man he had the rare opportunity to study with Taoist *I Ching* master, Master Khigh Alx Diegh. Upon completion of his initiation into this ancient wisdom tradition he was instructed to live, for no less than thirty years, before undertaking to teach new initiates. And live he did.

In his twenties, William spent several years trekking through the Central and South Americas with his wife, Leonor, and had the even rarer opportunity to live amongst and learn from the indigenous Tarahumara of Mexico's Copper Canyon. Afterwards he and Leonor settled in Oregon where they raised their daughter and ran a transitionary shelter home for abused and neglected children. In this work William learned invaluable insight into human nature, the human heart and psyche, as well as what can only be described as the art of diplomacy.

Throughout his travels and travails, William has, through genuine intent and faithful practice, had the great fortunes of glimpsing through the veil of the human senses in the *tonal* to the true encompassing reality and mystical magic of the *nagual*. It was this intent and practice that prepared him, at the age of fifty-three, for his own temporary dying as a result of a massive coronary attack.

He returned to this life, however, to share what he has learned along the way, through his many books, including his autobiographical works *In the Oneness of Time* and *Facing Light: Preparing for the Moment of Dying*, his instructive text on *The Toltec I Ching*, co-authored with artist and Nahuatl scholar, Martha Ramirez-Oropeza, followed by his multi-volume *Researches on the Toltec I Ching*, as well as several volumes on divination, spiritual practice, and poetry.

Meghan Elizabeth Tauck lives with white, cis, heterosexual, class, and citizenship privileges within the white supremacist cisheteropatriarchal and capitalist social system of the United States. This truth has affected and continues to affect every aspect of her life and cannot be ignored or denied.

As a child, Meghan developed debilitating anxiety and depression and has lived most of her life under the stress and strain of the invisible disabilities of mental and physical illness. This truth has also affected and continues to affect every aspect of her life, and neither can it be ignored or denied.

Her personal struggles led her to study psychology (she received her bachelor's degree in Psychology from Lesley University) as well as various healing modalities, such as neo-Reichian characterology and group process, biodynamic craniosacral therapy, and wisdom traditions such as astrology, Taoism, and the *I Ching*.

Additionally, in her twenties, Meghan discovered a great source of strength and healing in putting her hands in the dirt and living in tune with the natural seasons. She has studied permaculture and ecology, and has spent the last decade building and running a small farm and homestead in Upstate New York.

Throughout her travails Meghan has maintained a fervent abhorrence for systemic injustice in any form and a commitment to developing her own integrity, working with others to subvert oppression, whether internally/psychological or externally/social, and supporting movements for collective liberation. She believes in the power and capacity of collective consciousness, self-awareness, and integral relationship to change the world for the better.

She has a Master's degree in Philosophy, Cosmology, and Consciousness from the California Institute of Integral Studies.

This is her first book.

Living in a Time of Dying

Cries of Grief, Rage, Love, and Hope

CHAPTER ONE

THE MYSTIC MANIFESTER

What has the future in store for this strange being, born of a breath, of perishable tissue, yet immortal, with his powers fearful and divine? What magic will be wrought by him in the end? What is to be his greatest deed, his crowning achievement?

Long ago he recognized that all perceptible matter comes from a primary substance, of a tenuity beyond conception and filling all space – the Akasha or luminiferous ether – which is acted upon by the life-giving Prana or creative force, calling into existence, in never ending cycles, all things and phenomena.

The primary substance, thrown into infinitesimal whirls of prodigious velocity, becomes gross matter; the force subsiding, the motion ceases and matter disappears, reverting to the primary substance.

~ Nikola Tesla
Man's Greatest Achievement
July, 1930

Arguably the greatest Manifester in the past several centuries of human history, Nikola Tesla dreamed inventions into the world.

As the above quote demonstrates, being a Mystic does not remove one from the world but, rather, makes one a greater conduit for bringing ethereal visions into the world of manifestation.

The basic experience of living comes down to two alternative worldviews: either *Existence precedes Essence,* or *Essence precedes Existence.*

Whether or not you relate immediately to either of these alternative worldviews, your life is nonetheless governed by one of them—

Existence precedes Essence means that matter exists first and all life and therefore mind emerge from matter. Obviously, this is the basis of the materialistic worldview.

Essence precedes Existence means that mind, or spirit, exists first and all life and matter emerge from mind, or spirit. Such is the basis of the spiritual worldview.

If you experience yourself, in other words, as a physical body that has developed consciousness, then you feel on some rudimentary level that matter gives birth to life and mind—and that the inevitability of your body's death signals the end of your consciousness.

If, on the other hand, you experience yourself as a spiritual being that has taken material form in a physical body, then you feel on some rudimentary level that spirit gives birth to matter—and that the inevitability of your body's death signals the return of your awareness to the spiritual realm.

In the first case, you identify with being mortal. In the second case, you identify with being immortal.

The spiritual viewpoint is exemplified by the *gnosis* of classical Neoplatonic thought, where all phenomena emerge from *The One*—

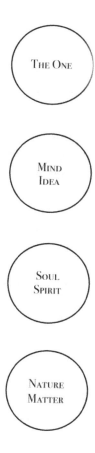

According to this schema, the realms of manifestation emanate from the ineffable *One* in a series of increasingly denser substance, finally manifesting in the world of matter.

In Taoist cosmology, we find a similar concept of emergence:

Tao gives birth to the One,
The One gives birth to the Two,
The Two gives birth to the Three,
The Three gives birth to all phenomena.

~ *Tao Te Ching*, Chapter 42

If we go back and re-read the quote by Tesla, we note a few points worth dwelling on:

- Human beings are mortal, yet immortal
- All perceptible matter comes from primary substance
- Primary substance is beyond conception and fills all of space
- All of space is the Akasha or ether
- Primary matter is called into existence by creative force, manifesting as all things and phenomena of gross matter
- When creative force subsides, gross matter disappears and reverts back to primary substance

Because the human body is a phenomenon, it is composed of gross matter—of breath and perishable tissue, as Tesla says. It is mortal.

Yet human being is also immortal, with powers both fearful and divine—how is this so? Because the physical body enters the world of gross matter only because its original, inconceivable being of primary substance is acted upon by the Prana, or creative force, inherent to the most sublime and imperceptible Akasha, or ether.[1]

---

[1] In various schools of Hindu philosophy, Akasha or ether is the fifth physical substance, which is the imperceptible *One*, *Eternal* and *All Pervading*.

The gross matter of the body returns to the primary substance when the creative force subsides and the body dies. But what of the "other part" of humanity that is immortal? Where does it go upon the death of the body?

Tesla does not state this explicitly but the inference is that this "immortal half" is the creative force itself, an individuated aspect of Prana, whose dwelling place is eternally the Akasha, or *light-bearing ether*. From this, we glimpse the worldview of the great Manifester-Mystic: the creative force animates subtle substance, giving rise to physical phenomena.

You, in other words, are the immortal, eternal, invisible *creative force*, which, through an act of *intention* has acted upon the inconceivable primary substance so as to call into existence your physical body.

Comparing Tesla's schema to that of the Neoplatonists' emanations reveals their underlying similarities—

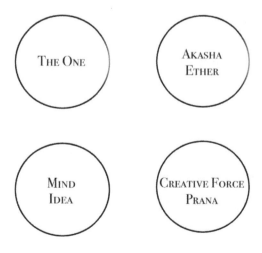

Tesla began having out-of-body experiences in his youth. Later in life, he dreamed some of his inventions down to the minutest details, using his eidetic memory to reproduce them in his schematics. His visualization skills were extraordinary, allowing him to envision his inventions in his mind, turning them over, opening them up, seeing them in every dimension, before building them. The full list of his discoveries is incredible, including the *alternating current* that powers electrical systems everywhere throughout the world.

You do not have to withdraw from the world to be a mystic.

You do not have to disdain physical existence or abstain from bodily enjoyment to be a spiritual being.

In fact, the opposite is true.

Real mysticism reveres nature and humanity as much as spirit. It is fully embodied within the senses, an ecstatic awareness filled with wonder at the miraculous actuality of its own physical existence within Creation. Its reverence manifests first and foremost as *nature mysticism*, the utter immersion and participation in Universal Life as it expresses itself in the natural world.

This mystical communion with nature extends to embrace all of humanity, as well. To return to Tesla's example, for a moment: he sought to develop a means of providing free electricity to all people in the world—the kind of goal expressing a kinship with people that seeks to make their lives better in meaningful and practical ways.

Such kinship is often described as radiating from a profound sense of *service to life*, a pouring forth of deep intention to *benefit all*.

Thought, or Idea, does not really extend into Intention until it has moved from the head, so to speak, into the heart. Intellect, in other words, does not manifest as Communion until it has been translated into Pure Emotion—a heartfelt selflessness that sheds every last vestige of perceived separation from all beings, both material and immaterial, in Creation.

Nor does selflessness express itself as deprivation. Rather, it blossoms as a living moment of shared ecstasy in the universal communion of The Many participating in the perfecting dance of time as it inevitably manifests the creative intention of The One in eternity. The *ecstatic life*, then, embodies the ancient teaching—

—for it experiences all the material forms of Creation *as* spirit, *as* the living Essence of spiritual reality giving rise to the living Existence of material reality. Moreover, the ecstatic life *celebrates* the living moment by consciously participating as an immortal being immersed in the sacred rite of mortality.

From this perspective, each of us is a divine being *engaged in a single continuous act* of encountering all the other divine beings in the world and treating each in a manner embodying our common divine nature.

Those who know that *Essence precedes Existence* identify with their immortal nature, experiencing themselves as deathless beings come into the realm of matter in order to be of service to Life in its ever-evolving act of manifesting its intrinsic perfectibility.

We come here, then, to work—to be the eyes and the hands of The One: the eyes, in order to experience mortal life of Creation from within; and the hands, in order to continue the perfecting activity of Creation from within. Our work, therefore, makes each of us a Manifester—no less so than Tesla, each of us is a conduit through which flows our own unique contribution to the Great Work of Creation.

So, we come here to work, yes.

But ultimately, we come here to die. To experience death for the sake of Life. To bring immortal understanding into the realm of mortality. And to bring mortal experience into the realm of immortality.

In the mystic's worldview, our mortal life is an act of self-sacrifice, an act of devotion, an act of love—our part in the sacred rite of fulfilling the vision of perfection that gave birth to the universe.

In the mystic's worldview, to live authentically is to live fully aware of mortality every moment, fully aware of always and everywhere *living in a time of dying*.

Chapter Two

Becoming Worthy of Survival

In my twenties I started learning to farm—to grow food and medicine, raise livestock, to live with the seasons and save for winter. I did this for two reasons: one, I found joy, pleasure, and personal healing in having such an intentional relationship with the earth; and two, I anticipated the eventual collapse of civilization and I wanted to be able to feed, clothe, and medic myself, my loved ones, and my community—I wanted to survive.

Back in the two-thousand-aughts, if I'd said that last part out loud most people would have laughed my concerns off as hyperbolic, the anxious delusions of someone with a history of mental illness. Many still might. However, a mere decade later, at the time of this writing, the catastrophic effects of global warming along with inequality-driven economic depression appear much more imminent and have become much more difficult to ignore.

Most people would agree that we cannot go on living the way that we have been—(especially those of us in the global North, which is responsible for using a disproportionate amount of the earth's resources)—even if they insist on maintaining optimism about these systems righting themselves after some not so gentle policy changes. If only we can oust the corrupt autocrats from positions of power and vote the right people—*good* people—into public office, then we can turn this thing around, they say. And while I commend their optimism (and I do concur that everyone should vote and push governments and corporate industries for substantive social change), I fear we may be a bit past the point where such social endeavors alone can adequately affect the necessary transformations in time for us to stave off the inevitable. Striving for social change at the institutional levels is simply an equal and opposing force to the powers of the status quo—the one exerts pressure upon the other in equal measure, ad infinitum. They are two sides of the same coin of what we have—consciously or unconsciously—manifested as our current social reality.

But that is not the only reality—there is another: that of the realm of *the Imaginal*, of *psyche*, in which we *dream* the manifest world into being. So long as we only attempt to affect change in the manifest, external, social realm we will simply continue in a never-ending cycle of opposing forces warring interminably against one another. In other words, we will simply perpetuate a paradigm of *war*.

Rather, every action that we take in the manifest world must originate from within the wellspring of the Imaginal. It must be rooted in spirit and nurtured in the soil of the individual psyche. This is how we may—individually and collectively—dream a new world into being that actualizes a new paradigm for how to relate and live together in the manifest realm rather than simply perpetuating an "us" versus "them" cycle of division and resistance.

That old paradigm is killing us. It is fundamentally what has led us to this dire precipice of a moment. We need to not only "think outside the box"—we need to get rid of "boxes" and arbitrary borders altogether, and take a different tact of *feeling* instead of thinking. Thinking is the modus operandi of the external realm; feeling is the language of the psyche, of the Imaginal.

Thinking is also the tool of time—it analyzes this moment from the next moment from the last moment, always anticipating an unknown future while concretizing the half-known past.

Feeling, on the other hand, is the perceptive organ of the eternal present. What we feel is always *now*, immanently vital, and thus eminently adaptable. One cannot change the past nor predict the future, and thus thinking about either, while invariably captivating, is nevertheless inevitably futile. The *felt present* is the only reality which we have any recourse to affect. Thus, it would seem that we had best embrace—and allow ourselves to be embraced by, enveloped in—the *feeling* of *this* moment.

~

It is the height of summer now, as I sit and write this on my farm in Upstate NY. I usually love the summer—I barely tolerate the harsh Northeast winters just to make it through to revel in the glorious heat and humidity that brings the rolling hills and valleys of my beautiful and sacred home into lush abundance. But this summer it hasn't rained much and the grass in the fields is brittle and chewed down to nubs by my hungry cattle as they leave dusty hoof-prints in the cracked earth beneath. All my vegetables are stunted and the berries small. We ration water between the garden and the livestock.

13

Of course, the birds still sing and the crickets are chirping their constant late summer hum. There is water in the creek that runs to the falls and down into our Finger Lakes. The falls have not quite run dry, not like in some recent years past. It's been worse, and is worse still in other parts of this country, and the world. I am so grateful for my green corner of the globe.

And yet where once I reveled in the beauty and vigorous abundance of a Northeast summer, now I cannot enjoy its unfurling generosity of this season without it being tinged with a deep sadness, the knowledge that all this—my beloved sacred home—is more or less slowly burning alive. Though it may seem slow relative to the perception of days or months, less slow in terms of years, and in fact quite alarmingly rapid by decades—including just the span of my own short life— and by the clock of history of life on Earth the raising temperature and subsequent loss of ecological stability leading to the sixth mass extinction is but the blink of an eye. An eon gone, in a geological instant.

It seems that every day I read another news article reporting that the bees are dying faster due to chemical pesticide pollution, or that the polar ice is receding faster than presumed, that portions of the Arctic—that great frozen tundra—or the Amazon rainforest—the great lungs of the world—are on fire, that this year is now the hottest on record, up from last year and the year before that, and on and on and on.

It is too late. No amount of recycling or driving electric cars or buying local is going to stop the tide that's coming—the tide that's already here. Such efforts in sufficient measure, and along with robust social support programs and drastic international

14

cooperation could help stem the tide (and should be undertaken immediately), but they won't stop it. By many estimates this world may be mostly uninhabitable for humans by the end of this twenty-first century, and some suggest this may come sooner, within only decades.

This is what I see and feel when I look out at the trees around my house, and my cows grazing languidly in the parched field below. Every time my heart opens to my beloveds—be they this land or its inhabitants, the bugs and frogs, the birds and opossums, the steadfast plants and wise old mycelium, the nourishing waters, all sacred beings—I feel them softly whisper, *Goodbye*, and feel myself reply, *I'm sorry*.

I'm only human. And so I must sit here, puny and ineffectual, my only recourse to *feel* it, my Love inextricably yoked to my Grief.

~

Meanwhile, the world is rising up against the powers of racial capitalism and colonialist exploitation which have brought us to this brink. From the jungles of Brazil to the streets of Hong Kong, from Palestine to Portland, from the fires raging across Australia, California, the Amazon, and Arctic to the unseasonably strong storms ripping through the Gulf of Mexico, middle America, Europe, South Asia, and on and on and on: the forces of this world that have been systematically exploited and brutalized for the profit and benefit of a very few have reached their breaking point.

Survival for survival's sake is no longer worth turning a blind eye in obeisance to the status quo, for the simple reason that it has become less and less possible to do so the way things are. Our "modern" way of life, based as it is on the exploitation and abuse of finite resources, including living bodies, is not only not sustainable, but it is neither ethically nor physically feasible— put simply, it should not exist.

Some have known this all along. Indigenous populations have experienced not only the wholesale and systematic destruction of their cultures, languages, and ways of life, but the calculated genocide of their peoples. Their very continued existence has been an act of resistance against the death-cult of racial capitalism and colonization. They have been warning us all along about the existential threat posed by such a dominant and exploitative system. But we were too busy and distracted trying to "get ahead" *within* such a system, never stopping to consider that any form of success in a fundamentally violent and exploitative social order necessarily means not only the tacit condoning of and complicity in the violence and exploitation against nature and other people, but the *direct* support and perpetuation of same. We didn't stop to realize that playing by this system's rules turns *us* into the *perpetrators* of that very system of violence and exploitation. Pure and simple.

"The system" cannot be said to be only "out there," in the world or up on high, but is "in here," within our own psyches, so long as we prioritize our own survival and well-being—our so-called "success"—at the expense of others, nature, and the global, collective good. And even if we recognized "the system" for what it is, and even if we struggled under the crippling weight of it—even if *we* are also those exploited by it—as long as we

16

deign to fight over the scraps dangled before us by such a callous, inhumane, divisive social structure, then we are participating in our own collective dehumanization and destruction. No modicum of "survival" should be worth that.

For the last 150 years we in the global West have been captivated (pun intended) by the Darwinian concept of "survival of the fittest," presuming a biologically natural imperative of competition between individuals. Never mind that this was a gross mischaracterization of Darwin's theory of evolution which conveniently supported an economic system based on inequality and exploitation, as well as a cultural preponderance towards individualism and the socially devastating tactic of "divide and conquer." But look where such an ideology has brought us—to a fractured, fragile, and imminently endangered global civilization, warring endlessly with one another while the rich get richer, the poor get poorer and more desperate, dissidents get arrested, beaten, and murdered or disappeared, and our global ecosystem and social fabric becomes increasingly tenuous.

We need a different relationship to survival, not one that emphasizes and rewards the individual at the expense of the collective, but one that prioritizes the cohesive, interdependent safety and fulfillment of all. And that cannot happen if we continue to uphold policies and acts of violence and exploitation against *any being*. It cannot happen unless or until we join with the forces of nature and humanity that are declaring "no more" and relentlessly pushing back against those powers that _must not exist any longer_.

The Black feminist author and activist Audre Lorde famously wrote that "you cannot dismantle the master's house using the master's tools." We must lay down the master's tools of violence and division once and for all, starting from within ourselves—from within our very own hearts, to the ways that we relate to and interact with others and our natural environment, to the actions and choices that we make. The struggle is not "out there." It starts with each of us "in here," in our fundamental relationship to our own selves, in our fears and insecurities— principally of death and aloneness. Our willingness to not only face and reckon with those fears and insecurities, as well as other exiled parts of ourselves such as shame and vulnerability, opens us to experiencing compassion, forgiveness, acceptance, trust, and love for ourselves and all beings, without reservation.

This is where *Meaning* is found; this is what makes life, and the world, *Matter*. And this is how we may—indeed, must—live in a time of dying. In truth, it may be the *only* way to really *live* in a time of dying, rather than merely *survive* in a time of dying— which is really just another way of dying in a time of dying.

We can no longer accept our divisions, narratives of superiority and inferiority, of "us" versus "them," "survival of the fittest," as natural or normal. They are lies. And they are killing us. Either we merely survive divided in a time of dying or we thrive together in a time of dying. There is no other option. I prefer the latter.

I prefer to face this time—and what a time it is to be alive!—in the full embrace of what this universe has to offer. That means accepting it, the world, others, and myself—ourselves—for who and what we are. It means accepting this time of dying for what it is, even as we also accept the responsibility to work for the transformation and betterment of all.

I cannot have such acceptance, nor truly accept responsibility, if I cannot feel compassion and empathy for myself and all beings in our most painful expressions and experiences; nor if I cannot hold myself and all beings in the grace of forgiveness for the ways that we have succumbed to a devious system under impossible circumstances; nor if I cannot hold to the truth that I am, and we are, eternally safe, held and protected in and by the spirit that imbues all things and all people, even as I face the most dire crises of embodied existence on this earth; nor if I cannot imbue my every thought, word, and action with the universal life force energy of love; nor if I remain closed to any facet of living and continue to relate to the world, others, or myself as fragmented, threatening, or either more or less worthy of respect and existence.

This is the fundamental crisis of our time that continues to cause trauma and suffering on an unconscionable scale: *that the existence of some is considered to be unworthy and thus expendable*. It is this violent disjunction that causes almost irreparable violence not only to the bodies of many, but to the souls of all, and to the very Soul of the World. It is the attempted *dis-memberment* of the world borne from the illusion that such severance is even possible—that we are not, in fact, inextricably One.

We must instead *re-member* that we *belong* to each other, and in so doing become *worthy* of survival.

CHAPTER THREE

ANAMNESIA

The nature mystic's vision is borne on the wings of an absolute faith in the transcendental power of self-sacrifice.

Even those who hold on to that belief through thick and thin, however, are sorrowed by the fact that the whole of creation is based on one thing eating another in an endless cycle of suffering and exploitation.

Of course that's what catches our eye at first. But for the nature mystic, the *light* of the fire has none of that suffering in it—it's in the fire itself, in the heat consuming the wood, that all the suffering is found. This means that all the sorrow is in the great bonfire of creation, the unfathomable cycle of life and death, the unquenchable wildfire of mortality, whereas the real transcendent presence of *pure spirit* is in the undying light emanating outward from that bonfire.

Such a vision keeps its gaze fixed on the pure and perfect light produced by this fire—keeps its ear attuned to the immortal song of joy and self-sacrifice produced by this roaring bonfire. It attends to what the fire of creation is *producing* and not just to the fire itself—to the light and song of immortality and not just to the fuel and fire of mortality. To do so makes it apparent that everything that suffers and dies *wanted* to come here, *chose* to

21

come here, in order to produce this perfect radiance of deathless ecstasy.

The land itself is spirit. If we do not collectively revere it and its plants and animals and climates, then we will splinter and compete among ourselves for advantage and wound the land for many generations to come. Spirit is freedom in every sense.

Similarly, if we don't collectively exhibit self-control, then the state will use it as an excuse for totalitarianism. Even under the best of circumstances, the state will use divide-and-conquer tactics to splinter us and encourage competition among us and wound civilization for many generations to come. We are all peers. All cultures are created equal. Nations and states are abominations, artificial constructions that can be unmade by people as easily as they were made by people.

Without such artificial constraints, the universality of spirit would inevitably be reflected in one perfect civilization—one not only at peace with itself but in harmonious co-creation with Nature, as well.

Nonetheless, for the individual, nothing is so necessary as to identify with the immortal awareness accompanying matter-energy across eternity, and not with the individual lifetime. Truth begins where it must end: either we act like rabid animals or we act like beatific angels. For this is the truth of free will: there is no human nature to discover—it must be created, by choice, out of its alternative. We can destroy ourselves or we can create ourselves, but we cannot help choosing: neither by words nor by imagination do we commit our energies to the creative forces, but by our intentional acts. Only when we decide that we are immortal and indestructible spirit can we be benevolent and just.

Every culture is created equal. Cultures are organic evolving creations. Governments, on the other hand, are artificial appendages affixed to culture. They cannot survive without culture, but culture can survive without them. For this reason, they are constantly contriving to spread their tendrils deeper into culture, trying to outlive the generations, creating the illusion that they are an intrinsic part of the real world.

But they are not. Just as culture cannot survive without nature, governments cannot survive without culture. We create them and we can un-create them.

In a world of peers, who has the right to dominate another? Do we really need alpha-males of our pack? Do we really need queens of our hive? Governments make themselves necessary by starting wars with other governments, dragging their peoples into the hell of unending hatred and revenge. They provoke and legitimize violence of people upon people. Like an addiction, they create a problem that they then seem the solution to. Is this the world we choose to live in?

How long must we live with this madness upon us? A nightmare from which we are able to so easily wake? Why are we lead about by the most brutish among us? When will we believe in the universal fellowship of humanity? When will we act on that belief?

These are the questions that we here feel no longer need be asked, for they have been answered with finality by the future generations. The past has had its hearing and we are grown deaf by its scream to perpetuate the past. It is governments who write history and teach us to keep the cycle of revenge going. So it is culture that must respond, taking up the burden at last of writing the future.

Do you remember being somewhere else before all this? Where there was enough for all and society existed to afford every individual the opportunity to fulfill their potential and it was all about creativity and loving-kindness and there was no violence or hatred anywhere? Do you remember being part of a whole whose continual bliss was indistinguishable from your own? Do you never wonder why we come into the world expecting to find just such a place? Why don't we enter the world expecting bared fangs and raking claws? Why does injustice and inhumanity cause us outrage? Where does the expectation of goodness and truth and beauty come from?

Never mind that those expectations are naive and cause people untold problems when faced with real-life circumstances— Where does that naiveté come from?

CHAPTER FOUR

THE PURPOSE OF LIVING

I recently found myself in the circumstance of having to euthanize one of my goats. She was an old goat, though not, perhaps, at the furthest reaches of her life span. I had had her for ten years, gotten when she was only a three-month-old kid, along with her two older sisters, Muerta and Venus. I named her Gemini for her spunky youthful spark.

Muerta—who had been a real favorite of mine—passed away only a few years later, tragically, from an incurable disease. Venus continues to live, fat and happy, as the matron of the herd. I guess it really does matter what's in a name.

Gemini was a purebred Nigerian Dwarf goat, and the runt of the litter at that, so she always remained small. She was a bit skittish and standoffish (and quick!)—didn't like to be handled, and would always keep just out of reach—but she was also curious, and would always come to see what treats I might be offering, or what the hubbub in the barn was whenever I would come to shear the pygora or trim hooves, as I do twice a year. She had the sweetest little high-pitched bleat: "meh-eh-eh-eh-eh," she would say, staccato, just like that.

Gemini started to flag a bit in the last year. She became thinner than her herd-mates, and a bit more reticent to enter the fray at mealtimes. Goats can be quite rough with one another and generally give as hard as they take, but Gemini being the smallest and one of the oldest, and having grown increasingly weaker, became less and less aggressive in advocating for herself at the grain troughs. I suspected she had worms.

Kept in captivity and forced to graze on grasses, rather than roam far and wide in forests and on cliff edges as they would in the wild, goats are perpetually beset by intestinal and various other pernicious parasites feeding off their warm red blood cells, causing anemia and general weakness, or attacking the lungs or spinal column and brain. Rule-of-thumb states that 20% of the herd will carry 80% of the parasite load, and in my case, with ten goats, one of those two was Gemini. I treat the herd twice a year with copper, which can help to keep the worms at bay, as well as administering a medical de-wormer to those goats who are the most susceptible.

Upon noticing Gemini's general malaise I began keeping a closer eye on her, worming her more aggressively, and supplementing her food with iron and other vitamins and minerals to help support where the worms were taking more than their fair share. We also fed her separately from the other goats, making sure that she got plenty of grain in addition to the pasture and hay forage that was always available.

And she bounced back! She became stronger, though she was still a bit thinner than I would have liked. She began going back into the barn at mealtimes and pushing her way in to the feed trough with everybody else. We were hopeful, but also wary.

We knew that Gemini's "time" might be coming, despite all our attempts at mitigation.

One morning we found her laying out in the paddock, in a pile of hay, tongue lolling. We thought that she was already dead but upon hearing her name she listlessly lifted her head. She was still with us, but definitely in trouble.

I lifted and carried her into a stall in one of the barns where I sat with her head in my lap as we waited for the vet to arrive. We hoped that it was something simple and treatable, like a case of bloat, and were hoping she might perk back up after some intervention. But as the minutes wore on, that became less and less likely.

Sitting there, alone and quiet, stroking my sweet struggling goat's sable salt-and-pepper coat, I became aware that there was nowhere I would rather be, nothing I would rather be doing.

A busy farmer and graduate student, my days at the end of summer—in the height of the harvest and with the new semester fully underway—had been almost impossibly full. It seemed I always needed to be in two places at once, doing at least four things at a time. But not now. Now everything stopped in a quiet, spacious, clarifying calm. This, in truth, was what it was all about, the purpose of this thing called living. All that other stuff—the due dates and appointments, the homework and papers—was merely a distraction, a million arbitrary ways of marking time, of marking "progress." Perhaps less so the tending to the garden and putting away food for winter, which is in itself an act of caring—but here, with Gemini, I found myself face-to-face with the crux of it all in stark relief.

27

I recognized in that moment—and really, not only re-cognized, but viscerally *felt* through every cell of my being; you might say I re-membered that—

> *I am an enfoldment of the universe showing care and respect for this goat-form enfoldment of the universe in her time of pain and struggle; I am, as such, an enfoldment of the universe showing care and respect to itself.*

That is it. That is the point. All else is superfluous.

And so, sitting there with my dying goat, I recognized—or re-membered—that despite the momentary pain and suffering of my dear goat, or the fear and sadness of a possibly imminent death, that this moment is perfection. Nothing to be done, nothing to be changed, nothing more important or valuable or immediately pressing—just the gentle quiet presence of *being with* in the moment, and perhaps especially in the moment of dying. This, right here, is what we're here to do. This is what the universe is for.

CHAPTER FIVE

THE ART OF UNLEARNING

People of the world learn day by day.
People of Tao unlearn day by day.

~ *Tao Te Ching*, Chapter 48

It takes a lot of work to free ourselves of the undue influence of others. Family, society, culture, history—all contribute to our personal experience of the *Zeitgeist*, the Spirit of the Time. And it is precisely our personal experience of the *Zeitgeist* and our reactions to it that inform our personality—indeed, it is everything we learn that informs our sense of identity.

At least until we unlearn it.

The horrors of the world are surely enough to drive us to despair, made many times worse by the scope of the horrors and our individual powerlessness to impact them directly.

Worldly knowledge teaches day by day that wrongs must be fought on their battlefield: political wrong-doing must be fought on the political battlefield; social wrong-doing must be fought on the social battlefield; economic wrong-doing must be fought on the economic battlefield. The problem with this approach is that it creates a predictable backlash: *reacting in kind* to wrong-doing creates actions that are perceived as wrongs by those with opposing interests, values, and intentions. Difficult as it is to admit, such efforts contribute to the cycle of action-backlash-reaction-backlash that reinforces and perpetuates the polarization of people. Ultimately, this plays into the continuing cycle of revenge holding people apart.

Mystical knowledge, on the other hand, teaches moment by moment that imperfections must be transmuted on the field of spirit—

A rabbi in the fourteenth century known for his mystical worldview was once asked for the secret of life and reportedly answered:

Everything is God. Live Well. Die Easy.

What "secret of life" is such a saying supposed to reveal? What relevance does such a "mystical worldview" hold in these times?

Actually, it articulates an ideal which, if universally followed, eradicates intentional wrong-doing before it arises. This it accomplishes by instilling within every individual true *peace of heart*.

When *everything* is recognized as divine, after all, that does not just include beautiful diamonds and crystal-clear rivers and sparkling snow-capped alps and purple-orange sunset clouds and iridescent hummingbirds and playful otters and loyal dogs and purring cats and perfect glowing newborn children and perfect glowing ancient wise women and men. No, it also includes wasps that lay their eggs in a living caterpillar so they might hatch and the larva consume the caterpillar alive, eventually eating their way out and leaving a corpse full of holes. No, it also includes mosquitos carrying diseases that maim and kill those they infect. No, it also includes frogs and snakes whose poisons attack the nervous system of their victims, dissolving tissue as it travels through the body. No, it also includes cowbirds who lay their eggs in other birds' nests so that they are raised by the unsuspecting foster parents even as they shove their foster siblings out of the nest and to their death. No, it also includes earthquakes and hurricanes and tornados and volcanos and wildfires and tsunamis that kill thousands every year. No, it also includes children who pull the wings off insects and emotionally torment other children. No, it also includes adults so filled with greed, hate, and self-loathing that they do not hesitate to perpetrate unconscionable acts of physical, emotional, and mental violence against others. No, it also includes all manner of disease and suffering that can be inflicted upon young and old alike. No, it also includes old age and the inevitability of death. And, no, it also includes periodic plagues and pandemics that lay low millions.

When *everything* is recognized as divine, in other words, the world is not seen as a *human* world. This extends further, of course, to recognize in the gamma rays and black holes and earth-shattering meteors outside the earth that the universe is not a *human* universe. To recognize that *everything* is sacred, is divinity itself, is to step outside our conception of what is preferable to human beings. It is to recognize that the universe, and in particular this earth, is part of a miraculous Creation full of characteristics that extend far beyond the spectrum of human

31

comfort and preferences and survival. Beyond, too, the scope of our senses—from the astronomical infinite to the subatomic infinitesimal, from dark matter to dark energy, from the interior of black holes to the interior of stars, our perception of Creation is prejudiced by all that *eludes* our human senses.

When *everything* is recognized as divine, we grasp the unitary nature of light and dark, good and evil, life and death, right and wrong, health and illness, and all the other polarities of our human-centric view of reality as *concurrent elements in the body of the divine*. It is not that we revere good or evil, therefore, but that we *revere the living body of the divine*. It is not a matter of judging things by their compatibility with human beings but, rather, of *revering the living body of the divine reality of which we are an integral part*. It is not a question of identifying with human beings, in other words, but of *identifying with the totality of the divine whole of which we are part*.

When *everything* is recognized as divine, all doubts are resolved in the greater paradox of the ancient formula, *As Above, So Below*, which establishes the fundamental relationship of the microcosm to the macrocosm: this relationship of the part to the Whole grounds the lived life of the mortal individual squarely in the experience of *being the body of a divine being within the Body of the Divine Being*.

We cannot say what this Divine Being is, for its true state of being is beyond the realm of our conception. But we *can* speak to its presence in this world of the five senses, for we *can* conceive its Body—

This world is indeed a living being endowed with a soul and intelligence . . . a single visible living entity containing all other living entities, which by their nature are all related.

~ Plato

If the etymological roots of the word *philosophy* promise the *love of wisdom*, Plato fulfills that promise two thousand years ago in his immortal description of the World Soul.

Can you *sense* the intelligence of this world? Can you *sense* the presence of this world's soul? Can you *sense* this world as a living being? Can you *sense* this single visible living being that contains all other living beings? Can you *sense* the nature of all living beings by which they are all related?

This is not a matter of conceiving something in mind. Rather, it is a matter of direct, primary awareness of reality—a stepping back into our intrinsic awareness that precedes thinking and words in order to encounter the living presence of the world through our own living presence. Such is the nature we share with all living beings, the nature by which we are all related and contained within the single visible living being.

This is what is meant by *Everything is God*: it includes us.

It is also what is meant by *Live Well. Die Easy*. To *sense* our own divine nature is simultaneously humbling and exalting—humbling, for we directly experience the grandeur of the divinity of The One of which we are part; and exalting, for it lifts us out of the experience of a separate being alone in an alien, inhospitable world, and into an eternal landscape of sacred

Creation. In this conscious experience of universal divinity we find ourselves in a state of grace, blessed with an ongoing upwelling of bliss that both encompasses and transcends all the vagaries of mortal life. Having reawakened our true nature to its authentic ecstatic state, we *Live Well* as deathless beings incarnated in service to the Whole, and *Die Easy* as immortal beings returning to our Universal Home.

This animistic-mystical worldview is not restricted to any one spiritual tradition. It lies at the root of every religion, spiritual tradition, and practice of self-liberation, making up the esoteric experience upon which their exoteric teachings rest.

In the soul's animistic-mystical worldview, we throw ourselves into the River of Time and encounter all the joys and sorrows of worldly existence. The existence of suffering and cruelty in a divine creation has long troubled humanity. Those who lived in earlier times confronted the same soul-wrenching questions from the perspective of their respective cultures and times. For example:

Why is the world as it is?
Because this is how God makes souls.

This world-making vision of the Creator embodies the archetype of the blacksmith—repeatedly heating mortal metal in the fire of spirit, pounding it into shape on the anvil of experience, and cooling it in the water of love—in the act of forging a mortal being into an immortal being. From the mystic's point of view, there is a meaningful spiritual logic to the idea that all of worldly existence creates stronger, wiser, more loving souls by dint of experiencing the heights and depths of mortal life. It does not ignore or negate the trials and tribulations of life. Rather, it incorporates them in a deeper appreciation of Creation as the Divine Forge within which the mortal lifetime is ennobled and sanctified, in keeping with the ancient alchemical formula—

The hotter the fire, the purer the gold.

Such is the mystical worldview.

You may of course be skeptical and more than a little incensed by such naivete.   And filled, moreover, with righteous indignation: how can murderers, rapists, child molesters, tyrants, and all the other myriad evil people in the world be considered divine? How can plagues and childhood diseases and senility and meaningless accidents and natural disasters be called divine? You may well feel that all this merely reinforces your view of "mysticism" as impractical and irrelevant to the real world, the product of overactive imaginations and an inability to accept the harsh realities of life. Certainly, this is an entirely valid perception from the *Existence-Precedes-Essence* worldview fostering a materialistic approach to life.

From the *Essence-Precedes-Existence* point of view, however, it seems fixed on what Gurdjieff called our "monkey cells" and what the Taoists call our "physical endowment." By this is meant the reactivity spawned by our instincts, especially for physical survival, which are triggered by what we perceive as threats.

What we perceive as threats is a matter of individual and cultural perspective. And "culture" can mean specific groups within a larger culture—for instance, some within a nation might perceive climate change as a threat while others do not, just as

35

some might perceive a change in social regulations a threat to their individual freedoms while others do not. The more complex that civilization becomes, the greater the variety in sensitivities to perceived threats.

All this boils down to the central question of *How are the wisdom teachings applied effectively to the times in which we live?* Because the sad fact is that sometimes we are confronted by very real threats to our individual and collective wellbeing. There are, of course, no universal answers as to how we ought to respond to such threats—circumstances must be addressed uniquely according to the values and role we hold at the time. This is never more apparent than when we are confronted with violence, oppression, or subjugation: one of the most difficult teachings to accept is that *There are no fixed mores in this world.* This example of Taoist philosophy is based on the recognition that what is an appropriate act at one time is deemed inappropriate at another time; and, likewise, that an act considered unthinkable at one time is deemed absolutely necessary at another time.

How do we confront wrong-doing without doing wrong? If we cannot have a universal rule that defines right *action* under such conditions, can we nonetheless define the *attitude* with which to act?

There does seem to be a narrow path through the thicket of thorns.

To the animist-mystic, it is found in this guiding principle:

> *Because everything is sacred, so are my own rights.*

For those dedicated to living a spiritual life, this principle marks a turning point of conscientious discernment and intention: to treat all things as divine is also to treat my own rights as divine— to treat the life and wellbeing of all things as sacred is also to treat my own life and wellbeing as sacred.

Not more sacred than others. But no less sacred than others, either.

This seems self-evident to the materialist, who treats the issue as a straightforward matter of social-political equality. But for the mystic, the matter runs deeper, needing to be resolved on the level of spiritual authenticity.

We come here to work. *To Benefit All.* To serve life in all its forms and manifestations. To care for the souls of all we encounter.

> *No stranger to trouble myself, I am learning to care for*
> *the unhappy.*
>
> ~ Virgil, *The Aeneid*
> 1st Century BC

Herein lies the need for wisdom. Without life-experience, we can fall into the trap of arriving at facile answers that treat the happiness of others as more important than our own. This is the result of the hard work of spiritual practice, which cultivates the deep and abiding sense of humility without which all service is tainted by egoism.

Not to put too fine a point on it, but without humility, *helping* others is too often done from a position of superiority, unconsciously placing oneself above the other. The act of *serving* others, on the other hand, is authentically accomplished by placing the needs of others above our own. This act of serving the Whole, of self-sacrifice to Benefit All, is considered the highest ethic of responsible action, placing the best interest of the community above self-interest.

The trap of naivete, of course, lies in mistaking the self-destructive desires of others for their true need, for their true best interests. This manifests in our taking a position of being "non-judgmental" or practicing "unconditional acceptance" of behavior that impinges on the sacred rights of others' lives or our own. This is where good-heartedness and good intentions must be rooted in wisdom: without clear-minded discernment and stalwart dedication to values sacralizing the Whole, we miss the opportunity for effective and timely response to destructive behavior.

Spiritually-minded people often think in terms of "lessons" they are meant to learn in this life. Certainly, this is not far from the ancient perspective of life being a soul-making forge, the ordeals and trials of which teach us to act compassionately, honorably, and courageously in the face of adversity—and to nurture the same in others.

But sometimes the lesson is not ours alone, for we are placed by circumstances of fate and duty to be the instruments by which others must learn *their* life lessons.

We are at our best when we are not outraged by the injustices done to us, but by the injustices done to others. It is understood that this *others* includes not just people, but all life, every life, and the sacred environment all call home.

*The war between good and evil
is fought on the battlefield of each person's soul.*

Though it is impossible to envision a universal rule for responding to wrong-doing, we can envision our goal: *to act without creating a backlash.* This is an art in itself. How to set things right without evoking resentment or anger—an art requiring deep understanding of human nature, true empathy and concern for the other's wellbeing, as well as impeccable communication skills.

When conflict of any kind cannot be avoided, wisdom seeks the path of least backlash by taking into account before action the potential for revenge it creates.

We can think of this by weighing the problems we eradicate against the new problems we create. Problems are not simply judged by their number but, more cogently, by the intensity and longevity of the potential backlash they generate. We must, in other words, beware: the cycle of revenge is difficult to interrupt once it gains momentum.

Wisdom speaks in the language of endings because without endings there is no change. This is especially true on the grand scale of humanity, whose collective unconscious cannot shift without ending its exploration of the darker side of human nature. Only after it has cornered itself through its pursuit of individual and group dominance, trapping itself in a living nightmare of self-destruction from which there is no waking, does it spontaneously accept that the inevitable end to this World-Age has arrived.

This eventual *positive backlash* of the collective unconscious is part of the deep structure of wisdom's language. Change moves from end to beginning to end again in cycles of human metamorphosis. Since ancient times, wisdom's language has embodied the *Universal Civilizing Spirit*, that most coherent radiant awareness that consistently exerts its subtle influence to awaken the individual and collective unconscious from their sleepwalking state. The *walls of sleep* form a progressive set of barriers holding individuals and groups back from awakening to full embodiment of their birthright of radiant awareness.

Wisdom speaks in the language of endings because without endings there is no starting over. Ending things in the right way at the right time brings about mutual understanding, forgiveness, and reconciliation—all precursors to a new beginning of building trust, acceptance, and mutual benefit. So long as the past remains an *object of continuity*, ingrained thoughts, emotions, and memories keep surfacing to prolong division, discord, and distress. The *Art of Starting Over* is one of *feelings*—it is an emotional backlash to the prospect of remaining stuck in a living nightmare forever. Its *art* lies in triggering the most meaningful ending possible and then riding out the repercussions as the new equilibrium asserts itself.

The potential for such a positive backlash lies in evoking a collective *Change of Heart*—the result of a global ending that affects the mythic, archetypal, collective unconscious of human nature, allowing a nearly universal catharsis of obsolete views and beliefs. It is as if everyone at once realized they had been navigating by the wrong star and, as one, changed course in the right direction.

Herein lies our present dilemma: we can see the tsunami disaster coming and we know that what *makes* it unavoidable is the behavior of human beings.

There have been, in other words, tipping points in the past that afforded us every opportunity to avoid this end. But human nature prohibited us from acting when we could have avoided overpopulation, climate change, environmental destruction, mass extinction, institutionalized inequality and injustice, perverse distribution of wealth, cycles of hatred and revenge, widespread hunger and lack of drinking water, competition for resources and political dominance: our instinctive drive toward self-interest proved stronger than our free will—we were unable to place the survival of the species ahead of our individual self-interest, thereby undercutting the very foundation of individual survival. For acting against the best interest of the species must inevitably eradicate the necessary support upon which every individual relies—just as destroying the natural environment upon which our species relies is the ultimate self-destructive act.

It is a perfect storm. There have been plagues and pandemics before. We could have weathered this one in a manner that resulted in much less suffering and loss of life. But all the other factors contributing to social division and competition added up to a collective failure of nerve to collaborate and cooperate in the best interest of the whole.

Individuals have, of course, sounded warnings along the way. Just as individuals continue to take up the work of stemming the tide of irrationality fueling our impending doom. But such efforts, absent the positive backlash to this self-created ending, prove futile against the overwhelming crush of the collective

41

denial of consequences that continues to govern our species behavior.

And herein lies our quest: *how do we act in the face of this looming ending?*

CHAPTER SIX

ON GRIEF, RAGE, LOVE, AND HOPE

For some reason I have always been deeply afraid of loss. I haven't suffered a great deal of it in my life (my first big grief wasn't until my dear old cat died when I was 14 years old), and yet somehow I feel intimately acquainted with Grief. It's almost as if the Grief in me is innate, inborn, perhaps a residue of a past life (or lives), a memory so deep and ancient it knows no origin or limits. Perhaps it is not even mine, this Grief that runs like a river just under the surface of my being. Perhaps it is simply one small part of a sacred message which we are all made to carry together, though alone, that communicates to us just how precious is this half of existence.

Did you know that existence has two halves? It does, as, by extension, does every individual thing, being, or moment in the manifest universe.

As do you.

And I.

Everything has its visible half and its invisible half: half in the physical-realm and half in the dream-realm. Both halves exist simultaneously, of course. They must. As primordial polarities,

43

one cannot exist without the other, which means nothing can exist without both.

The visible half includes everything that can be sensed (or *felt*) with any sort of apparatus, organic or technological, from subatomic quantum events to the vast contents of the all-encompassing Universe. Its polarity—the invisible half—on the other hand, cannot be said to include anything at all; rather, it simply *is* the raw undifferentiated potency of everything that ever could be. It is the *dream* of the world, of the vast contents of an all-encompassing Universe, of you and me, and what *could* be. As such, there *is* no loss from the perspective of the invisible half, because there's nothing to *be* lost! Only from the visible half do we suffer the pain of loss, the overwhelm of Grief when something or someone so dear to us, and that can never be replaced, ceases to exist in this embodied realm.

And so perhaps Grief is simply a love letter from the beyond, from the potency that yearns for manifestation, and which can only find purchase in meaning through the fact—the raw tragedy and gift—of life and death, reminding us tenderly of what we have: the preciousness of the mere fact of embodied existence of every being—every entity, every molecule, every event—in this manifest universe. Perhaps, despite our Grief, or nay, *because* of it, we know that *we* are the lucky ones.

This is why I have such a deep respect for Grief. It is the truth; it is honest. There is no shame in Grief, no reason to hide from it. Because Grief is Love's lover. The two walk together, hand in hand, inseparable. As soon as I love someone Grief is just right there, on the other side of the veil of loss. And like Love, Grief is a beautiful and terrible emotion which has the power to fill me up past my breaking point, until I feel like I must burst, for it seems impossible that I might be able to contain my Grief (or my Love) within such a small, finite corporeal form.

It may be terrifying, thus, to love someone—or, indeed, this world—and face, intrinsically, the loss of them. But isn't that an expression of the best, the most courageous in each of us—our ability and willingness to open ourselves and share our lives with another? This is the seat of our very humanity. Each person, each being, each moment which touches us, our lives and our hearts, is a gift. And so too is the Grief that comes when they pass away and are no longer with us. We carry this gift with us, always. It keeps us tender; it keeps us honest. It is how we know that we are still alive and still not afraid to love.

In her poem, "In Blackwater Woods," Mary Oliver wrote the now famous words,

> *"To live in this world*
> *you must be able*
> *to do three things:*
> *to love what is mortal;*
> *to hold it against your bones knowing*
> *your own life depends on it;*
> *and, when the time comes to let it go,*
> *to let it go."*[2]

Truer words were never committed to ear, paper, or binary code. Herein lies the crux of it. "To *live* in this *world*," in visible embodied existence, we must be able to *love* what we know will

---

[2] *New and Selected Poems, Volume One.* Beacon Press: Boston, 1992, p. 177.

inevitably, nonnegotiably die; to do so knowing *our own life* depends on the finite fleeting life of our beloved; and yet be prepared and willing to let go our beloved when that cursed hour of our eternal parting *must*—as it always must—finally come. This is Grief. But this is also Love. The twain walk ever hand-in-hand, never the one without the other.

This is what it is to live. Because this poem does not merely speak sentimentally about the love and loss of another; this poem at its core speaks about the very relationship of the soul to the beloved corpus of the body, its vehicle in the realm of the visible half of existence on earth. "To live in this world" the soul, that potent undifferentiated spirit of the invisible formless realm, must become yoked to a finite and transient body through its yearning and pure love for that which exists in form, and without which it, the soul, the invisible spirit, could not exist and is thus utterly dependent. And yet despite the penetrating depth of yearning and love, and its utter dependence upon the embodiment of the visible realm, the soul must be willing to give up its beloved embodiment, let go its corporeal existence, the very object of its deepest yearning, and relinquish itself, its own life, back to the nothingness of undifferentiated potency—back to the invisible dream.

This is the grief we face in the passage of every moment, never to be had again. Every moment is, itself, precious—is the unique expression of the vast unfolding, unfurling cosmos through the existence of every individual being. And thus, while each moment, and each being, must pass away in its time, this does not negate its inherent value, its worth to the unfolding manifestation of the Whole. Each moment and each being deserves respect, deserves to be honored in the fullness of its integrity, its own wholeness.

Herein erupts the Rage when such is not observed, when we witness harm being done to other beings—be they individuals or whole societies, whole ecosystems, the body of this unique and integral planet itself. We *feel* that such callous, wanton, and willful harm goes against the very nature of nature, against the fundamental Love and reciprocal dependence between the visible and invisible halves of existence. "To <u>*live*</u> <u>*in*</u> <u>*this*</u> <u>*world*</u>" we must be able to *love this world*, to hold it as *precious* and *irreplaceable*, even as we prepare, from the deepest reservoirs of our courage (literally, *coeur-rage*, the *rage* of the heart, a *Rage* based in *Love*), to let it go when our time comes.

And yet we see everywhere people being mistreated, abused, exploited, held in chains, raped, murdered, and starved; we see capitalist tycoons pillaging the earth's natural resources and the lives and bodies of workers for the sole purpose of meaningless economic profit; we see species upon species of animals, birds, amphibians, fish, insects, and plants being pushed into extinction as their habitats are steadily demolished to make way for modern life; we see the skies and oceans, forests and soils polluted and denuded, rendered poisonous wastelands where once they were the very lifeblood and manna of this richly dynamic teeming earth system. These ways are not how "to live in this world"; these are ways of dying. They call us, like soldiers to the great battlefield—or, rather, like medics, those courageous heroines of our darkest hour—to summon our *Grief* and our *Rage* to the service of tending to those being fed unceremoniously through the veil of loss as through a woodchipper, and to the protection of all we hold dear.

47

Because, like Grief and Love, Grief and Rage, too, go hand-in-hand, like a yin-yang of sadness and anger constantly turning the one into the other. Grief begets Rage at the injustice of death, and Rage protects the tenderness of Grief against the onslaught of pain in the face of it.

But Grief is not simply the agony of loss, the price we pay for having opened ourselves to Love. Rather, the function of Grief is to make meaning of the meaningless, to sacralize the incomprehensible pain of loss to death. Faced with such a cosmic injustice—the irreversible loss of that which we love and which cannot be replaced, as the very bones of our own bodies and from the very core of our beings—we must *make it sacred*. It is in our Grief that we declare, "Have a care, here is something that matters!"[3]

Meanwhile, the function of Rage is to give us something yet to live and stand for in those moments of inconceivable, inconsolable Grief, lest we ourselves dissolve away into that ever-yawning abyss. And that *something* is the protection of what remains, of what yet matters still. Grief and Rage, rooted as they must be in Love, call us to the breast of the World-Soul, the one for comfort in the wake of loss, the other for courage to endure it nonetheless, or all the more.

But either would become all-consuming and wreck devastation upon and within us if it were not for one more necessary ingredient: *Hope*.

---

[3] Gratitude to philosopher Alfred North Whitehead for this phrase: *Modes of Thought*. Capricorn Books: New York, NY, 1958 [1938], p. 159.

I confess that Hope has, at times, seemed to me like a four-letter word, a luxury that I could not afford in such times of utter despair. To hope, I felt, rendered me vulnerable to the crushing blows of disappointment and heartbreak each time I witnessed, again and again, the harm and injustices meted out against the beings of this world.

I have also seen Hope used as a cudgel and as a chain—the criterion of bearing Hope under hopeless circumstances used to silence and stem either the power of Rage or the wisdom of Grief.

But Hope is not the same as optimism—it does not necessarily mean that we expect things to get better, or to be saved, or for some utopian future to arise without injustice, exploitation, or violence. Hope is not simply a passive wish; rather, Hope is an active response to suffering and injustice. Hope is an act of *resistance* to the callous wanton death-cult of imperialist white supremacist cisheteropatriarchal capitalism[4] and *protection* of all the precious living beings under threat in its wake, which, at the end of the day, is *all* of us. Hope is not compulsory; it is a *choice*. Hope is facing hopelessness and taking action anyway, continuing to live out every day with all the integrity, courage, love, and compassion that we can muster. In this way, Hope is what keeps us dreaming a new world into being.

Hope is the knowing that this is not the way that things should or have to be, that we *can* do and be better—to ourselves, one another, and the planet—and that we deserve to live in a world

---

[4] Thanks to Black feminist author and cultural critic, bell hooks, for coining the basis of this phrase.

that respects, honors, and supports us *all* to live in (and live out) our fullest capacities as unique expressions of the unfolding unfurling cosmos.

That is what I hold onto when the Grief and the Rage threaten to overwhelm me. But my Hope is necessarily informed by my Grief and by my Rage. Without Grief, Hope is mere sentimentality, coerced through the drivel of platitudes; without Rage, Hope is toothless, the frivolous privilege of empty promises. And without Love, all is meaningless.

CHAPTER SEVEN

FANGS AND CLAWS OF HISTORY

The conscious and intelligent manipulation of the organized habits and opinions of the masses is an important element in democratic society. Those who manipulate this unseen mechanism of society constitute an invisible government which is the true ruling power of our country. . . . In almost every act of our daily lives, whether in the sphere of politics or business, in our social conduct or our ethical thinking, we are dominated by the relatively small number of persons . . . who understand the mental processes and social patterns of the masses. It is they who pull the wires which control the public mind.

~ Edward L. Bernays,
Propaganda (1920)

No matter how dark I think it is, it is always darker.

Have you heard of Operation Paperclip? This was a U.S. military operation at the end of World War Two that had its counterparts in the Russian and British military. These three nations went into a defeated Germany, divided up the Nazi scientists and intelligentsia, and took them back to their respective nations.

This is an historical fact. There exist photos of the group removed to the United States. Werner von Braun, father of the Saturn rocket that put men on the moon, was one of that group. These were Nazis and Nazi sympathizers, in other words, who were placed in positions of influence.

I do not wish to conjecture in what positions of influence they were placed. I merely wish to point out that the United States did not ever strive to be a superpower or dominate the world militarily or politically until after World War Two.

And point out that such is all the United States and Russia have thought about since then.

Germany may have lost the war but that does not mean the Nazis did.

There is a saying: when corporations control government, that is fascism; when government controls corporations, that is socialism.

I cannot say if that is precisely true or not—political theory is not my wheelhouse. It seems to paint a complex picture with broad strokes—and generalizations always risk over-simplifying. On the other hand, sometimes it can be clarifying to strip complexities down to their essential relationships.

The battle, then, may not really be "capitalism vs socialism" as much as it is actually "fascism vs socialism."

Any time nations experience a rise in nationalism, persecution of immigrants and minorities, widening of class and wealth disparities, authoritarianism, political propaganda and disinformation campaigns, etc., then its citizenry ought to be alert to the very real possibility that fascist tendencies are brewing right before their eyes.

In the midst of crises that have no simple solution in sight, people run the risk of placing their trust in figures and institutions that project strength and promise to return to an idealized past.

The dream of world domination does not arise among the people of a nation—ordinary people have no interest in such things. It is a dream of the powerful few who are able to influence politicians and set a nation's foreign policy over the course of decades.

Although it does not arise among the populace of a nation, the dream of world domination creates governments that become increasingly authoritarian within their own borders. Totalitarianism requires compliant citizens: if one is to dominate the world, one must first dominate one's own people.

CHAPTER EIGHT

THE ROAD IS PAVED WITH FEELING

All that is *is* an expression of Feeling. What we experience we do so through Feeling; perception is Feeling, the qualitative valuation of experience, and thus Feeling is the foremost, the primordial, the first mode of perception. Thought is secondary. We feel things first, then we think about them.

This has been a significant point of inquiry—and contention—in philosophical discourse since the time of Plato. For well over two thousand years thinkers have wondered at the "stuff" of reality, what makes our world and the universe what it is and us what and who we are. In the global West, beginning at the time of Plato and Aristotle and reaching its zenith with Descartes' "Cogito Ergo Sum"—"I think therefore I am"—thought or *logos*, rational interpretation, has been elevated to the highest pinnacle of existence in the world, if not the universe. It is assumed that the singular evolutionary apex is the human mind.

The rest of the universe, world, and nature has been presumed to be simply inert matter subject to the mechanical forces of physics and/or, in the case of animate life, the instinctual forces of biology—both are ultimately mechanistic and paint the existents of this world as mere machines, distinguishable only by their relative complexity (for example, a gazelle is more complex than a plant is more complex than an amoeba is more complex than a rock). Humans alone occupy the upper echelon of the evolutionary stratosphere by our unique capacity to reason, to objectively observe and to analyze and interpret the world in which we exist. This is what we call "consciousness," which has in many ways become synonymous with self-awareness—it is our capacity for consciousness that allows us to have a concept of self as opposed to an "other," of an "in here," subjective experience, distinguished from the "out there" objective world or reality. And so we are able to think—"in here"—about the world "out there."

This capacity has given us tremendous insight into, as well as control over, how the world works—including scientific discoveries of physics, chemistry, evolutionary biology, and ecological systems, as well as, more recently: human psychology and behavior; social contracts, law, and systems of governance; symbolic representations through artistic and linguistic expression; and, of course, spiritual and religious conceptions of divinity and the various ritual and organized practices of worship. All of these fundamental expressions of human culture, society, and ingenuity stem from our capacity for abstract thought.

However, abstract thought is just that—abstract. The function of thought is to dissect, discern, and discriminate "this" from "that," subject from object, the "inner" self from the "outer" world, "us" from "them," so that we can name and thus know— or more precisely, know *about*—"them," the world "out there." There is nothing inherently wrong with this function—in fact, it is essential to what makes us human. A problem arises, however, when this thinking-function is deemed superior to and thus divorced from the feeling-function that directly perceives the inherent connectedness and interdependence of all things. Because in the abstraction of the thought process all "things" become objectified. Thinking about the world, or anything within it, necessarily distances us from that "thing," that "object," and thus from the world which we wish to observe and to know.

Have you ever tried to observe something—anything, from a bug or a leaf, a moment in time, or even the full breadth of your sensational perception—without *thinking* about it? Without a descriptive or analytical thought or narrative arising in your mind?

To be able to do so is the holy grail of meditation practice, and it is the bane of most "civilized" people. Because we can't do it! We are simply not practiced at not thinking. Thoughts about the world or life, about our experience of living, invade our minds in a constant stream.

What we find when we are able to set our thoughts aside—like an obedient puppy sufficiently subdued from barking at the clouds passing overhead—is, to use the words of philosopher William James, a world of "pure experience."[5] Everything floods in, nothing is filtered out, dismissed or ignored, as our perception balloons out to include the whole of experience in its fullness, positively buzzing with dynamic vitality. And we are in it, we are indistinguishably a part of that vibrant buzzing wholeness. We are no longer locked away "in here" peering out at the living world "out there" as if through plate glass; no, we

---

[5] *The Journal of Philosophy, Psychology and Scientific Methods*, Vol. 1, Nos. 20-21 (1904).

experience ourselves, we *feel* ourselves, as an expression of the fullness of nature, the fullness of life, the fullness, even, of the unfolding universal cosmos.

But thought is a feature (not a bug) of being human, and so inevitably, even with much practice, this penetratingly profound experience of enveloping immanent Oneness lasts only so long before we pop back into thought, back into the narrative stream—the puppy raises its head again to continue its aimless barking at the sky.

To think is surely important and central to our human experience and role on this planet, as much as are our opposable thumbs, bipedal structure, and capacity for complex speech. But it is not the be-all-end-all of what and who we are. And it is not the only (or indeed best) way for us to live in and interact with the world around us, of which we are a vital and integral part. Rather, when we resort to thought we become *apart from* the world before us, and thus "it" becomes merely inert matter for us to control and shape to our will and whim, no longer a dynamic, immanently vital Oneness of pure experience.

Thus, where once we lived and worshipped at the foot of the great trees that have fed and sheltered us for millennia, now we beget deforestation; where once we wondered at the majesty of mountains and strove to scale their peaks, now we beget mining for resource extraction and mountaintop removal; where once we worshipped the sacred life-giving power of water, now we use it as a global toilet, polluting the hydrosphere with toxic sludge and fumes—waste products from resource extraction and manufacturing of so-called "goods"; where once we lived in relationships of reciprocity with the flora and fauna with whom we share this world, and on whom we also depend, now we enclose, abuse, and exterminate them for our own gain through intensive and concentrated farming practices, habitat destruction, and suburban sprawl; where once we lived in relative egalitarian harmony with our neighbors, now we fear, hate, subjugate, and exterminate them in the interminable conflicts and hostilities that breed violence, slavery, systems of dehumanization, war, and genocide.

Thus we get a civilizational death-cult.

Thus, where once we lived for the gift and grace of our survival, of our very existence, now we spend all our days, all our time, all our resources, thrashing against our own sacred existence and, simultaneously, the knowledge of our impending demise. And in so doing we participate in the perhaps inadvertent if not wanton demise of that most gracious gift which cannot be replaced. Thus we get living in a time of dying...

Our thinking, our rationality, may be an inherent and necessary tool of our humanity, one which is crucial to responding to this crisis of our own making, but we must remember that it is not the only tool at our disposal. Admittedly, feeling is not a tool we—perhaps particularly in the modern global West—are accustomed to or skilled at using. In fact, because we've so thoroughly ostracized and repressed our feeling-function, when we do use it we often do so in ways that are at best messy or worse, downright harmful. Observe: violence in the streets, or vicious virulent rhetoric swapped online, or reactionary defensiveness in response to confrontation. For this reason, and perhaps now more than ever, it can feel especially tenuous to lean in to our feelings. But it is essential if we are to meet the moment, the world, and ourselves with authenticity and integrity—if we are to meet *what is* with the full breadth of our humanity.

Philosopher Alfred North Whitehead writes that "the [primordial] form of physical experience is emotional—blind emotion—received as felt elsewhere in another," and, moreover, that "the [primordial] element is sympathy, that is feeling the feeling in another and feeling . . . with another."[6] In other words, sympathy—or more accurately, empathy, the capacity to *feel with*—is foundational to existence and, therefore, to all manifestations of life, from the smallest atoms and microorganisms, to the vastly interconnected planetary biosphere, to the relations of human beings with one another and our physical environment. Empathy—*feeling with*—is not a liability of who we are, but, rather, it is fundamentally *what* and *who* we are, and, as such, is a nonnegotiable necessity in how we live our lives. It is how we experience the dynamic buzzing vitality of ourselves—and one another—as inextricable expressions of an immanent divine whole, rather than as alienated, fragmentary, and finite entities apart from this great encompassing All.

For generations, Feeling has been increasingly denigrated in the global Western philosophic canon—and within the modern psyche—as a sentimental if not dangerous diversion from rationality, which is presumed to be the highest and best expression of humanity. But see where our precious Western rationalism has brought us: our thinking has laid open the world to our whims, yet in so doing it has brought us to the brink of

---

[6] *Process and Reality*. Free Press: New York, NY, 1978, p. 162.

extinction, to this time of dying. It has done so because it has been divorced from Feeling, from the sympathetic, empathetic, capacity that is not only the foundation of our existence and our humanity—and thus essential to our survival and continued existence—but is our *birthright*.

It is fundamentally who and what we are to *feel with* others, nature, and indeed the living soul of the whole world and cosmos. Such an experience of connection and Belonging— with those with whom we share this earth, our human and non-human relatives, and to a fundamentally caring divine universe—is our birthright. We should not and do not have to feel alienated and alone, ostracized and isolated, divided and opposed, detached, abandoned, and insecure. We *belong* to one another, to this earth and all its species, and to a radically loving, empathetic, divine universe. What's more, we are all aesthetic *expressions* of that radically loving, empathetic divine universe—we are all radically loving, empathetic, and divine beings. *That* is our birthright. It is our calling on this earth, and our true source of empowerment.

Our thinking-function may be a tool, but our feeling-function is the blueprint for what we want to build, for who we want to become. It is the map of the territory and the territory itself. We make the road by walking[7] and the road is paved with *feeling*. This is why, as we face this time of dying, we must have the courage to feel it: the Grief that comes from Love, the Rage that comes from Grief, and yes, even the Hope that arises despite (or perhaps because of) all three. Our empathy is our north-star; our

---

[7] Paraphrase from the poem "Traveler, Your Footsteps," by Antonio Machado.

feeling-function must be our guiding light in the darkness of the fear and uncertainty of these times, for it is the primordial, the most essential commonality which connects us all. And we need each other—all our relations—if we are to survive. And all the more to thrive.

CHAPTER NINE

UNCONDITIONAL SURRENDER

It has been a long time since far-sighted and humane individuals were accorded positions of large-scale decision-making. Such ancient societies took it for granted that the needs and welfare of the coming generations were as important to decisions as the needs and welfare of the current generation—a stark contrast to our long history of short-sighted, self-interested "leaders" stumbling from one avoidable crisis to the next.

There is little room for self-restraint any longer in condemning the degenerate heart-minds of those who put their own desperate life-negating desires ahead of the common good. Nor is there room any longer for optimism in waiting for those holding the reins of power to acquire a conscience and abdicate in favor of those who hold all life sacred. To wit, a demand for unconditional surrender—

Ultimatum

Either
All religions band together
Against all governments and command their every adherent
To cease forever every violent act, word, and thought
Immediately—

Or
They all be damned together for Eternity.

Those who foster and benefit from the desecration of nature—including human nature—are the last relics of the World-Age presently coming to an end. There are two factors, however, that are beyond their ken and will ultimately mark their final passing into forgotten history.

The first is their species-centric worldview—so encapsulated in their acquisition of material wealth, status, and dominance are they that they live their entire lives never having experienced the spirit of nature. Plato said of the *World Soul*,

> "This world is indeed a living being endowed with a soul and intelligence . . . a single visible living entity containing all other living entities, which by their nature are all related."

Initiates like Plato shine through the darkness of the past World-Age like torches keeping alive the fragments of wisdom teachings still surviving from the even earlier World-Age of harmony between nature, human nature, and spirit.

The second factor is the sea change in the priority given to the *relationships between things* rather than to things themselves. This increasing awareness of the inter-relatedness of all things results in a drastic re-prioritization of human behavior as it effects both the wellbeing of the environment and the coherence of human communities. Products and behaviors that negatively impact the environment and result in inhumane living conditions are no longer justified by desire, force, or privilege. Once people stop purchasing such products and stop behaving counter to their own interests, they alter both what is produced and the collective responses to circumstances. Acquiring things then takes a far-distant second place to nurturing the balanced and harmonious relationships establishing a coherence within the Whole—one that endures over the long term by remaining flexible and adaptable as circumstances change.

The spirit serpent sheds its skin every day.

What are we willing to let go of here at the end of this World-Age? What outgrown skin are we able to slough off in order to renew our love of Life and stave off as long as possible the inevitable end we now face? How much free will do we really have?

CHAPTER TEN

A CRISIS OF BELONGING

'I' becomes 'I'
when I have learned
my place in the group
when I become aware
of the fact
that my actions
have consequences
on others
on the whole
only then
am 'I' a person
A WHOLE PERSON
~ Viola F. Cordova,
"Who We Are"

We have a crisis of belonging.

Our crisis of belonging is due to a profound rent—an ideology of separation—by which we perceive ourselves as distinctly separate and disconnected from others, the living world, and the divine. This perception provokes a deep insecurity and fear within us that causes us to feel we must *confront* and be in competition with hostile others in an inherently threatening

67

world, and that in order to survive we must therefore exert whatever forms of power and control that we can over our immediate circumstances, our environment, and those "others" around us.

This is our reality. It is how we are taught and raised to experience our world, and ourselves within it: we are alone in a hostile environment and we must fight for survival against constant threats from outside.

By "we," of course, I am speaking primarily of those of us living—or dying, as the case may be—in so-called "modern" so-called "civilization," the hallmarks of which are the particularly Western belief in a bifurcation of "mind" from "matter," divine from the world, and human from the Earth. According to this ideology of separation humans claim a paternalistic superiority over nature, animals, and, indeed, other humans over which—or rather *whom*—they seek to exert violent power and control. Such a modern "civilization" is manifested through the ideologies of white supremacist racism and xenophobia, misogynist, homophobic, and transphobic cisheteropatriarchy, and capitalist imperialism and colonization, and exists now in almost every corner of the globe due to centuries of Western European imperialist conquest.

It is the development of this modernity and "civilization" that has come to afford those of us who are privileged by these systems the comforts and "freedoms" of modern industrial society, including various technologies, democracy, industrial agriculture, national identities, the ability to travel freely over vast distances, the opportunity to be educated in schools and universities, the legal and economic apparatuses that allow us to purchase and exchange, to own and to collect, and so on. However, all of these modern "advances" come at a high cost—they all depend in some way or another upon the exploitation of nature and other human beings, which itself depends upon the ideology of separateness, on a worldview that perceives and treats nature and other human beings, and ultimately oneself, as mere objects that must be controlled.

According to such a worldview—to such a conception and experience of *reality*—life and the world are both utterly devoid of meaning as well as profoundly alienating and perilous. Just as nature, we are told, is simply a mechanistic conglomeration of disparate particulates of dead matter spinning aimlessly through space, we, too, must exist simply as isolated individuals fumbling through life until the time of our inevitable demise in death. Such a world can only be experienced as cold, unfeeling, random, and meaningless.

As the late Apache-Latina philosopher, V.F. Cordova writes,

> "The [Western] reality . . . consists of seeing man as an isolated, potentially self-sufficient unit of existence. This model is manifest in the belief that man, the individual, is in competition for survival against every other man; he creates himself, not through others, but in opposition to others. Man is isolated from nature; he is superior to it. Nature is a hostile force opposed to human beings and ever ready to absorb the unwary individual [i.e. in death]. Nature calls him to succumb to its oblivion and man must fight this by continually striving

69

to 'develop' his isolation and self-sufficiency [i.e. control]." [8]

In contrast,

> "In the reality of most Native Americans, however, man is not an isolated and self-sufficient unit of existence. Man is a group being and dependent, not only on others, but on the Earth. Survival depends not on competition but on cooperation. Man is not a being in opposition to nature but a part of it. Nature gives him his subsistence; the group gives him his identity" [9]

The price, therefore, for our modernity, for our "civilization," is the loss of a sense of integration and *belonging* within a vitally immanent and deeply caring cosmos in which we are inviolably held in reciprocal interrelationship with all other beings; in other words, the loss of a worldview and experience of reality in which we belong to one another and the Earth itself.

This loss occurs by a process of *colonization* by or *assimilation* to the dominant conquering or occupying ideology, that of *individualism* and the separateness of beings from one another and nature, as well as of the divine from the world. In order to become "modern" and "civilized" we have lost, or given up by force or coercion, our innate birthright, the sense of belonging to a place, to this Earth, to a people, to a culture, to a history, to an eternally dynamic and immanently divine web of relations.

---

[8] Moore, Kathleen Dean, Peters, Kurt, Jojola, Ted, & Lacy, Amber, eds. *How It Is: The Native American Philosophy of V.F. Cordova.* University of Arizona Press, 2007, p. 122.
[9] Ibid.

And this loss is a *trauma*. To experience ourselves separate and alone, awash in an ultimately empty, unfeeling, purposeless, and futile existence is *traumatic*. It renders us powerless, insignificant, and deeply insecure. Such a worldview positions us—in relation to the world, others, and even ourselves—from a perspective of fear and *scarcity*. If the world and indeed the universe is empty and meaningless, and our own lives are insignificant and finite, then in order for us to survive—in order for us to go on living, to have the courage to wake up every day and face our own existence—we feel we must cling to whatever vestiges of surety and control that we can grasp.

Unfortunately, any attempt to control in this way is, inevitably, a violence. Whether we attempt to control the Earth and nature through technological advancements for resource extraction in order to ensure that we have food to eat, water to drink and wash, clothes to wear, tools to use, and shelter to call a home, or whether we attempt to control other bodies for the labor to extract and produce the goods we need to survive and thrive, or whether we attempt to control our own selves through shame and out of a desire—a *need*—to be accepted by others, i.e. to *belong*, we are committing violence. Thus, this crisis of belonging also *perpetuates* trauma by projecting it *outward* onto the world, and *inward* onto ourselves.

Hence the adage "hurt people hurt people," or, as contemporary American abolitionist activist, Miriame Kaba has been quoted as saying, "No one *comes* to violence as a perpetrator." We visit violence, harm, and trauma on others and the world because we experience it first within ourselves—either visited upon us by others who have themselves been harmed and traumatized or, ultimately, by acquiescing, by force or coercion, to the modern ideology of separateness and the fear that it engenders within us. Thus such fear and insecurity breed a mobius loop of trauma and violence, the only escape from which, I argue, is the antithesis to an ideology of separation, that is: cultivating—*re-membering*—a sense, an experience, of *belonging*.

We were all Indigenous once. But in the process of becoming "civilized" some of us lost our indigeneity, and in the course of colonization many of us have forgotten our interdependence within the web of relations in favor of a sense of a separate *individuality*. We have undergone a process of *dis-membering* and so we must learn to *re-member* our birthright.

It is important to note that I am not suggesting that we who have lost our indigeneity can "re-indigenize"—although perhaps, given enough time cultivating a civilization based in respect, reciprocity, and an abiding connection to place, but that is not for me to say. As Luther Standing Bear, an Oglala Lakota Chief, said, "Man must be born and reborn to belong."[10] However, what I *am* suggesting is that we would do ourselves and this world a great benefit if we *listened* to Indigenous peoples and followed their lead.

Of course, any discussion of indigeneity must not neglect the continued perpetration of forced land dispossession and exploitation. Those who maintain their indigeneity do so in resistance to violent occupation and the dominant social and ideological paradigm—they have refused to give in despite

---

[10] *Land of the Spotted Eagle* [1933]. University of Nebraska Press: Lincoln, 1978.

centuries of violence, land dispossession, cultural erasure, ethnic cleansing, and attempts at outright genocide. Cordova writes,

> "The indigenous American—despite five hundred years of concerted efforts by government, the military, and educational and religious institutions to eradicate a conceptual framework alien to the West—has managed to maintain a separate identity based on a conceptual framework that still seems to provide a better explanatory framework than that offered by the West."[11]

This distinct identity is based, she argues, in an ethic of respect for an other as *other*,[12] of the interdependent interrelationship and mutual reciprocity between the vast diversity of all existents, or beings, in nature,[13] and of an abiding *bondedness* to a group and "bounded space" or geographical place for one's sense of meaning [14] and identity. [15] It is the combination of these fundamental tenets that create a sense of what I am referring to here as "belonging."

The implications of such a worldview are that:

1) an other is one's equal, and hence a diversity of perspectives is fundamental to social discourse—thus differences are not to be assumed to be either inferior or dangerous;

---

[11] *How It Is*, 2007, p. 68.
[12] Ibid, p. 190.
[13] Ibid, p. 105, 184.
[14] Ibid, p. 73.
[15] Ibid, p. 194, 199.

2) we are all connected and need one another to survive and thrive—thus pure individuality, and especially individual*ism*, is a myth;

3) rootedness to a specific place and within a specific group and social and historical context is paramount to our identities—to knowing *who we are*—and thus to feeling empowered and secure to live fully, to express our authentic feelings, to dream and envision, and to take thoughtful and responsible action in and for not just ourselves (because there is no such thing), but for the collective whole of which we are part and on which we depend.

Thus, one cannot claim to possess or control, nor denigrate or exploit, by force or coercion, another being or natural ecosystem without concomitantly causing reciprocal harm to oneself and one's own continued survival. For there is no survival of the one without the survival of the dynamic whole; we thrive together or not at all.

This is what it means to belong. This is what provides an inviolable sense of *security* in the world, with others, in oneself, in the universal cosmos, and in this dynamic ever-changing dance called living. Such a deep abiding sense of security that comes with belonging in and to the web of relations counteracts the ultimate insecurity: the awareness that individual life is finite, even as the web of life continues eternally.

But in order for us to *re-member* our belonging we must resist and subvert on all fronts—socially and psychologically, in the world as in one's own mind—the contradictory tenets of modern "civilization" and the systems of social hierarchy and oppression

74

that uphold them. This is because indigeneity and the inherently violent, divisive, dis-membering establishment of white supremacist cisheteropatriarchal capitalist imperialism are mutually exclusive. An ideology of separateness, with its concomitant binary of superiority and inferiority, on which our modern "civilization" stands, is antithetical to an ethic of belonging.

The Indigenous throughout history have been forced or otherwise compelled to leave their homelands, forget their languages, and with it their worldviews, as well as their rituals, beliefs, and mores, and a deep abiding belonging to the Earth, spirit, their people, and a way of life—indeed, their very identities, along with their entire culture and civilization—in exchange for a much more tenuous "belonging" based on relative and entirely conditional requirements of membership and worth.

Rather than belonging simply by virtue of our existence, according to the modern worldview one must prove one's merit by the very stringent, hierarchical, and violent criteria of the imperialist white supremacist capitalist cisheteropatriarchal power structure. The world over, one is deemed more worthy of existing if they are white, light-skinned, or have European features; if they are a national citizen rather than an immigrant or refugee; if they are educated according to Western academic standards; if they control or have access to financial wealth; if they are cismale (born with male genitalia and live as men), heterosexual, and traditionally masculine (as opposed to effeminate); and if they adhere to the dominant religious, political, and ideological traditions and mores. The world over, those who exist outside of these standards—Black, Brown,

Indigenous, and Asians of varying ethnic and cultural backgrounds, poor and working people, immigrants and refugees (particularly those of color), ciswomen, lesbian, gay, bisexual, trans, non-binary, and femmes of all genders and sexualities, as well as Jews outside of Israel, Muslims outside of the Arabic world, Palestinians within their own land, and political leftists everywhere—are ostracized, isolated, persecuted, and subject to violence. But even for those afforded the privilege of membership status among the socially favored, it is a dubious acceptance at best, conditional as it is.

And yet for those in modern "civilization" who feel they have no other recourse to a sense of belonging, such membership is critical to maintaining some semblance of control in an otherwise chaotic and hostile world. They cling to it as if their lives depended on it, because, from such a perspective, they do. We who have lost our indigeneity and been taken in by the modern colonial ideology of separation and estrangement, with its celebrated myths of individualism and meritocracy, grasp and cling to whatever scrap of false power we might glean. And we protect it viciously, out of fear that it, too, may be rent away from us, and we become abandoned once more upon a vast and uncaring world.

Our fears are stoked by the very existence of "others," those unlike us who, by virtue of their difference, of their contrast to the rightness and righteousness of our own exclusive membership privileges, can only pose a threat to our superiority and thus to our security. For without our superiority, who are we?

Cordova links this ideology of separation, with its bifurcation of the human from the Earth and binary of superiority and inferiority, to the proliferation of Christianity in the West:

> "The view of man as a stranger on his own planet is only as old as Christianity. The idea that man's individuality is preeminent over his role in the group is only centuries old and that too can be traced to incipient roots in Christian thought. Euroman's treatment of human beings and of the Earth is essentially based on the views of man as an individual who is somehow superior to, or different from, the Earth."[16]

In a world bifurcated into dichotomies of superiority versus inferiority, of "in-group" versus "out-group," of membership versus ostracism, in which all are made to compete for power, acceptance, and survival, if one is not in a superior position then one must, necessarily, be inferior. Because all that we know, all that we have been taught by this worldview, this ideology of separation, is that "belonging" is dependent (by which I mean *conditional*) on one's in-group status, which necessitates that there be an out group, an Other, and that if we're not "in," if we're not superior, then we must necessarily be "out" and thus inferior. Such precarity of place, of inclusion and "belonging," engenders a deeply entrenched and visceral sense of *insecurity*.

This insecurity, and the fear it elicits, is rooted in the visceral emotional—or *felt*—experience of *separation*—from others, from nature, from God or the divine immanence of the cosmos, and perhaps most of all from our own sense of integrity, of

---

[16] *How It Is*, 2007, p. 52.

wholeness, within our own hearts and minds. And so we attempt to control others, and nature, and even God,[17] in order to ensure our continued, if illusory, security and superiority.

It is also why groups that peddle fascistic ideologies are so seductive, particularly in the West, to white, predominantly Christian, heterosexual cismen, those for whom the promise of superiority has been so great, and thus its falsity so disorienting. Humans are social creatures—we *need* to belong and to feel deeply embedded within a people, culture, and place for our identity, in order to know who we are. Those who have been spoon-fed the myth of individualism but are bereft of a sense of inclusion in and attachment to a people or place are easily taken in by the memberships offered by strongmen and demagogues. As Cordova writes, "An individual, set apart from his group, can be more easily manipulated by others."[18] Neofascist groups the world over offer just another form of membership based on separatism, violence, and control, because at least denigrating other people together can afford them a sense of bonding. But "bonding" is not the same as *belonging*; it is in this instance simply another form of bond*age*.

If we don't feel a sense of *belonging* then we feel ourselves simply drifting along without a bedrock on which to base an identity—it is as if we are zombies marching across a barren hellscape—and so we will seek out or create a sense of identity and "belonging" elsewhere.

---

[17] *How It Is*, 2007, p. 109.
[18] Ibid, p. 156.

This is perhaps no more apparent than with white heterosexual cismen because it is they who have been classified the heroes and champions of the dominant order of modern imperialist white supremacist cisheteropatriarchy, upon which they have based their sense of identity as superior to and thus in a position of control over the world and its inhabitants. Consequently, so long as there are "others"—people of color, Jews, Muslims, women, trans and non-binary people, leftists and "Commies"— who are not explicitly held in a subservient position, then the identity of supremacy of the white Christian heterosexual cisman is challenged. Because if those "others" are not in a subservient position then they must also belong, and so the possibility of their existence as equals shakes the fragile foundations of the security in superiority found in modern imperialist white supremacist capitalist cisheteropatriarchal "civilization."

This is perhaps the greatest tragedy and trauma of all: because we fear not "belonging" within the structures of power put in place by the imperialist white supremacist capitalist cisheteropatriarchal modern "civilization" we miss out on an experience of truly *belonging*. Because we feel those coveted conditional memberships to be so fragile, we use those very structures of violence and separation in order to maintain a sense of superiority over others, both by isolating ourselves from others and by perpetrating just such violence and ostracism against others through arbitrary and utterly useless narratives of hatred and bigotry. And because we also feel ourselves outside of and superior to nature, we feel entitled and emboldened to extract from and exploit the natural environment and its myriad inhabitants for our own physical comfort, security, and

79

accumulation of financial wealth with no sense of limitation, reciprocity, or responsibility, leading to the current situation of global ecological collapse.

The fragility of identities based on supremacy, on a relationship of exploitation and *power-over* rather than of reciprocity and *cooperation-with*, which are bred from a lack of a sense of deep abiding *belonging* to a place and a people, thus create with them a fragile world. And the acceptance and perpetuation of such a distorted and hurtful worldview as that which pits us against one another and the Earth, and even against ourselves, itself perpetuates and proliferates *trauma*. This trauma lives within the recesses of the individual psyche, it is traded systemically and generationally, and it is projected outward onto others and the Earth. The trauma is one of dis-integration, of fragmentation, of separation—of sanctioning with our complicity and thus recreating and being made to live in a world that has become deeply and perhaps irrevocably broken.

These are the consequences of our crisis of belonging.

But this modern ideology of separateness and superiority creates a false dichotomy that is predicated on a *misperception* of our reality.

In truth, belonging is not conditional—it is *non-negotiable*.

We all belong, always. That is our birthright. We are here, we exist, therefore we belong. And if we *feel*—deeply, viscerally—that we belong then we have no need of fear, and no recourse to social divisions or exploitation.

And yet it is through this misperception of our reality—that we are separate and must either be superior or inferior—that *we treat each other* as such.   In other words, we *create* such a reality when we accept and perpetuate an ideology of separateness, not only through the mechanisms of bigotry, social apartheid, and violence, but through our own allegiance to *individualism*, with its narratives of fear, scarcity, and alienation.

But it doesn't have to be this way.   It *isn't* this way, in truth.

In fact, we are not separate.   There is no individual—and no individual*ity*—that is not inextricably connected in a network of relationships of reciprocity with all other beings in this living world.   As Cordova states "there are no self-made persons. There are only those who cannot (or refuse to) acknowledge their debts."[19] We must acknowledge our debts to one another and to the greater living whole that is this planetary ecosystem.

> "[M]an is not an isolated and self-sufficient unit of existence. Man is a group being and dependent, not only on others, but on the Earth. Survival depends not on competition but on cooperation. Man is not a being in opposition to nature but a part of it.[20] . . .   It is time to see that humans are a part of the ecological web and that they too play a vital role—not as stewards over an inferior and mindless nature—but as a necessary part of a healthy and diverse system of life."[21]

Moreover,

---

[19] *How It Is*, 2007, p. 158.
[20] Ibid, p. 122.
[21] Ibid, p. 207.

81

"Human beings are not meaningless things in this universe. Their every act affects the universe. There are repercussions and consequences to each action. Humans, perhaps unlike other life forms, have a greater capacity for memory . . . This capacity does not make of the human something 'superior'... It makes humans more responsible. They alone can know and understand the consequences of their actions."[22]

What kind of world could be dreamed into being by a worldview based on the tenets of belonging—respect, reciprocity, and an abiding bondedness to both a people and a place? How might we relate differently to one another and our Earth? How might such a perspectival shift affect how we perceive ourselves, our identities, and our place within a dynamic and ever-changing cosmos? How might we *feel* differently about our own finite existence, or, indeed, our eventual non-existence?

We have a crisis of belonging.

We have lost a sense of what bonds us together, both as a people and to this Earth. We have been torn from one another and from the supportive, nourishing, life-giving ground that sustains us. We have been dis-membered. But we can re-member our birthright. We can re-member our sacred relationships. We can re-member ourselves—our deeply interwoven and interdependent identities, our integrity, our wholeness. We can re-member our *belonging* as the deep knowing and abiding sense of being fundamentally and unconditionally *loved* and supported—by one's human community, by the Earth

---

[22] *How It Is*, 2007, p. 212.

community, by the universe, and within the embrace of the divine, what my friend William Douglas Horden calls the Sphere of Universal Communion.

CHAPTER ELEVEN

DREAM A BETTER DREAM

What is the most tragic thing in the world?

Seeing a newborn infant, smiling and cooing contentedly, overflowing with joy, its eyes filled with light and open curiosity.

Why is this the most tragic thing in the world?

Come back in forty years and see what has become of that ecstatic infant.

Nothing more tragic, too, because of the despair of parents and grandparents, who delight in the fireplace glow of the infant's joy even as they know how short-lived its gentle flame is. Sheltering the infant as well as possible for as long as possible, the day comes when they must hand it over to the greater social life and then watch helplessly as every year diminishes the inherent joy of life with which their child entered the world.

The eventual result, of course, is an entire civilization of people who resemble domesticated horses whose wild spirit has been broken. Besides the war, violence, hatred, starvation, poverty, racism, bigotry, and systematic desecration of nature and human nature to which such broken spirits are daily exposed, there is the self-doubt and sense of meaninglessness they must endure as they increasingly confront a life devoid of opportunities to fulfill their heart's desire.

I ask you to imagine for a moment a different world—

A world in which all of human civilization is channeled into a single overriding priority:

To marshal all its resources into assuring
every individual is able to sustain the infant's ecstatic state
throughout the entire course of their lifetime.

Imagine for a moment what kind of world we would create if the only purpose of civilization was the perpetuation of the original state of joy of every individual, generation after generation into perpetuity.

CHAPTER TWELVE

ANOTHER WORLD IS POSSIBLE

It is asinine—this world.

In the U.S. alone (though certainly not exclusively) we have politicians using their power and influence to—

> stop queer people from getting married, or going shopping, or using the bathroom;
> force people with uteruses to give over their bodies and their lives in order to carry out a pregnancy;
> force immigrant children to flounder in cages and holding camps, rather than move freely in the world;
> stop Black, Brown, and poor people from voting;
> funnel resources always away from communities—from cities, towns, and working people—and into the pockets of a few corporate owners;
> force people to pay their hard-earned money to insurance companies who act as gatekeepers to even the barest modicum of medical care;
> send bombs and guns to kill and terrorize entire populations in order to secure and maintain control of economic assets, like trade routes and pipelines;

> continue to extract and exploit fossil fuels even as we experience rising temperatures, melting sea ice, raging wildfires and super storms, while countless people and species suffer...

Meanwhile, those of us not in positions of corporate or political power resort to dividing ourselves into camps, either for or against, and squabble over scraps according to antiquated zombie ideologies of separative supremacies with arbitrary borders, like race, religion, nationality, ethnic origin, political affiliation, and so on. We pit ourselves against one another, competing endlessly for righteous satisfaction while those running the show—those with the power to actually affect real people's lives—continue to make decisions and bend the wills and whims of history to their own best economic and political best interests.

Meanwhile, the world burns;

Meanwhile, people work their lives away yet still live in poverty and go without food, medical care, or shelter;

Meanwhile, people languish in prisons and holding camps;

Meanwhile, people suffer unconscionable violence and trauma...

It is asinine.

It makes me so, so sad.

Although "sad" seems too small and quiet a word to express the depths of despair and heartbreak wrought by the world we have created.

And make no mistake, we have created it. The circumstances we now find ourselves within were not put upon us by God. They are not the machinations of nature—even so-called "human nature." They are, rather, the *dysfunction* of human nature, a result born of millennia of pain, fear, and trauma.

To say that our global social circumstances are dysfunctional is, of course, to say that they are *not functional*. The current sociopolitical structures and ideologies that we have devised, which uphold (or hold down, depending on how you look at it) our human civilization—governments, economies, nations and borders, supremacisms, militaries and warfare—do not function to support us; they do not function to sustain us; they do not function to ensure our health and longevity, our quality of life, or our en*joy*ment, liberation, or peace.

To be sure, these structures and ideologies are functionally antithetical to human and ecological thriving, which is our sanction and birthright.

Rather than support, they exploit; rather than sustain, they extract; rather than health, they generate disease; rather than longevity, they ensure destruction; rather than quality of life, they offer exhaustion and alienation; rather than joy, they engender pain, trauma, and despair; rather than liberation, they require submission; and rather than peace, they promise perpetual conflict and war.

We have created such a world as this. And we can *un*create it.

We can dream a new world into being. We can endeavor to discern what of this world deserves to be kept and what should be dispensed with post haste. We can entrust ourselves to live in such a way as to accept self-responsibility, to respect and care for ourselves, others, and nature, to align with integrity rather than reactionary compulsions, to eschew supremacisms and arbitrary divisions, and to support one another to live full and fulfilling lives.

We can create a *functional* world in which personal and collective fulfillment, liberation, and yes, even peace, are not only possible but preeminently necessary.

The question is only: *will we?*

CHAPTER THIRTEEN

THE TIDES OF MYTH

To even speak about equality among all people is shameful.

Not that equality is shameful, of course. But to have to advocate for it or defend it here, two decades into the 21st Century—this is shameful.

To even have to think about it is degrading. It soils human nature to face the horrifying reflection staring out of the social mirror. The grandeur of human being—the indomitable will to discover truth and create beauty and feel love—and its potential for a humane and just civilization seems ever just-within-reach; but ever aborted by the basest and most wretched parts of the human soul.

It is shameful that at this stage of social and psychological evolution we still have this sadistic shadow not just hovering over us, but lurking within us—what a horror! What an abomination stares back from the mirror!

~

I lived for forty years in Southwestern Oregon, and like others living in a rural community, sooner or later had to deal with a septic tank in need of repair. The middle-aged gent and his

91

twenty-year-old son dug up the cover and opened the tank to assay the problem.

"It's clogged and has to be cleaned out by hand," he explained in a no-nonsense manner. "We'll wait for you to do that and then close it up for you," he continued, scuffing the ground with a well-used work boot. Evidently, he did business with lots of folks who didn't hesitate to climb down into the waist-deep muck themselves.

He interpreted my silence correctly. "Or my boy there can do it for ninety dollars."

There is an ancient saying in the *I Ching* to the effect that *When cleaning out a well, it is necessary to go all the way to the bottom.*

I wish I could report that it was I who donned the rubber suit and boots and waded into the backlog of my own shit. But I did not have the stomach for it. What I can report is that there was a young person strong enough and motivated enough and capable enough to do just that—for me.

~

I would not want you to think I have lived in a bubble. I spent the Sixties on the West Coast and experienced firsthand the corruption of the police. I went to school in Watts just after the riots there and saw firsthand the death of a Black teenager at the hand of a White security officer.[23] I spent more than twenty years running—and living in—a shelter home for abused and

---

[23] Detailed in the book *In the Oneness of Time*, Larson Publications, 2015.

neglected children. I have lived off and on in Mexico for years and seen the institutionalized oppression of people.

I suppose all the political and social issues, important as they are, pale in my own mind to the decades I spent living with and caring for abused and neglected children. From six months to eighteen years of age, all the children in the county that needed to be placed by the court for crisis intervention came across my doorstep. I saw close-up the traumatic effects of parental abuse and I understood that the dark side of human nature is unfathomably cruel.

But I also saw the light of resilience within those children.

In a way, I guess I see the cruelty of those with either power or the willingness to resort to violence as the same side of human nature as those abusive parents. And the victims of social injustice and oppression as the same side of human nature as the innocent children traumatized by the incomprehensible cruelty of others.

But I also see, of course, the resilience and strength and courage that such innocence inspires.

And herein lies the power of myth.

And the reason the tide of oppression is rising.

~

Obviously, *myth* is the story we tell ourselves about how to interpret the world—especially, how to interpret the *meaning* of things, the whys and wherefores of the events and actions around

93

us. Even more especially, myth reveals the hidden forces behind events, be those forces named gods or demons or enemies external or enemies within.

The reason the counterculture won the culture war of the '60s and '70s—even if only for a brief time—was because it told a more compelling myth: Peace and Love resonated with people's hearts more than War and Hate. It didn't exclude fellow citizens, many of whom were parents afraid of losing their sons to a meaningless war. It opposed political doctrines and corporate war profiteering. And it won people's hearts.

The failure of the counterculture at that time—and the reason it did not last—was that in cleaning out the well, it failed to go all the way to the bottom.

~

We can see that it is easier to construct a myth of victimhood for those bemoaning the loss of a better past. The flip side of that is that it is much more difficult to articulate a positive vision of the future in which all benefit.

My first teacher, a Taoist master, advocated publicly for a future in which every individual was a World Citizen, with the birthright to move freely in a world without borders and nationalities.

My second teacher, a Tarahumara shaman, taught that *If you love the world, it loves you back*. This was his direct experience of a living, intelligent world of nature aware of every individual life.

How that echoes Plato, who, in describing the World Soul, said *All things are connected and It has intelligence*.

~

We have the knowledge and resources to build something glorious. There is a Golden Age of Humanity out there just-out-of-reach, one of peace and prospering for all, a civilization at peace with itself and in harmony and balance with nature.

But we are going to have to climb down into the septic tank and clean out our shit. We cannot hire someone else to do it for us— there is no one else. And, most importantly, we have to go all the way to the bottom this time.

And, lastly, if the past few decades have taught us anything, it is that we will not have the stomach for that unless inspired by a positive myth that captures our imagination with its vision of a future whose rising tide lifts all boats together in greatness.

CHAPTER FOURTEEN

SPIRITUAL ANARCHY OR THE INNER FASCIST[24]

PART I

As I sit to write this, the United States is approaching the threshold of another fateful presidential election, the result and aftermath of which will no doubt be remembered for decades to come. Our country has not been so divided in over 150 years, not since the fight to end slavery set us on a course for civil war.

The side for abolition was victorious all those years ago...or was it? Since then, every politician, every administration, and every policy has had to answer to the bitter remonstrations of white prejudice against extending rights, privileges, and protections to Black Americans. From Reconstruction to the New Deal to Civil Rights to modern Neoliberalism, at every stage along the way efforts to advance social justice and egalitarian provisions for building a robust, equitable, and economically sustainable social order have been thwarted by white racial grievances against accepting the rights of Black people to exist in the national landscape except in a position of servitude.

---

[24] The following three-part essay is dedicated to my dear friend, my soul's companion, Che Broadnax, who helped coin the term "Inner Fascist," and whose friendship has taught me so much about the deepest parts of myself and about the true meanings of anarchy and freedom. I am eternally grateful for his love and comradeship. ~ M.E.T.

Consistently throughout United States history we have seen that white people, in general, would rather subvert our own social and economical protections, privileges, and benefits than cede any of the same to Black people. For all our so-called "post-racial" rhetoric there still exists a pernicious poison lurking in the shadows of the white American psyche: that deep (or sometimes not so deep) down we still believe that we are superior to Black, Brown, Indigenous, and other people of color.

Now, I can practically hear the white people reading this collectively scowling, huffing, and indignantly slamming this book closed. "How dare they?!" you might be thinking. "They don't know me; *I'm* not like that!" Or, perhaps you're thinking, "Why do they have to bring the issue of race into it?"

But the "issue of race" is here already, no matter what, whether spoken or unspoken. Because the fact is that Black, Brown, and Indigenous people of color are the ones who bear the brunt of the dying that we have been discussing in these pages, and which we are now experiencing across this planet. From strategically orchestrated widespread poverty and resultant malnourishment and starvation, to war and social conflict; to environmental destruction, land expropriation, and climate chaos; to mass incarceration, reservations, and ghetto segregation; to refugee camps and immigrant stigmatization; to modern slavery and labor exploitation; to lack of access to social supports, infrastructure, and health care; to social sabotage and attempted extermination through forced sterilization, denigration, and suppression of languages and cultural practices, and the calculated lure and accessibility of drugs and alcohol; to Islamophobic persecution and violence; to kidnapping children and forced family separation, the world over it is Black, Brown,

98

and Indigenous people—*especially women and transgender people*—who suffer the greatest amount of death and grief under the current imperialist white supremacist capitalist cisheteropatriarchal power structure.

As activist Malkia Cyril Devich says,

> "Death is a part of life, it's natural. But the deaths that we have been subject to as oppressed people, they're unnatural . . . We have an unequal relationship to death and loss. That's not natural. That's not okay."[25]

This is why we *must* say "Black Lives Matter," and why we cannot say that all lives matter *until* we see reflected unequivocally in our social policies *that* Black lives matter. Because according to a white supremacist dialectic, anti-Blackness is unavoidable, and as long as white supremacy and anti-Blackness exist as two sides of the same coin, all skin tones and characteristics of non-white peoples are subject to white supremacist/anti-Black denigration and violence. And we know that we are living under a white supremacist dialectic because even after 150 years since the abolition of slavery in the United States, this matter of the value of Black lives is apparently still up for debate. That is a disgrace. The statement "Black Lives Matter" is thus an invocation of a world in which all lives *do* matter and a declaration of the inherent value of life itself. As author and activist Layla F. Saad has said, "Blackness is the agenda that frees us all."[26]

---

[25] *How To Survive The End Of The World Podcast* with Adrienne Marie Brown and Autumn Brown, "Being with Terror," released Oct. 5, 2020.
[26] *Good Ancestor Podcast*, Episode #032, released Oct. 1, 2020.

It is not the first time, nor will it be the last, that we are faced with a choice between the legacy of white supremacy in the United States and a future in which Black lives matter. The North may have won the Civil War, but the South never stopped fighting.[27] Now, as those alive during this time may remember, we seem poised on the verge of another descent into social chaos and conflict.

Across the country tensions are flaring, and the foot-soldiers of white supremacist right-wing fascism, including armed vigilante militias and the police forces that protect them as well as the power of the state, are becoming increasingly emboldened, menacing, and violent towards anyone who stands against the current order. White supremacy has enjoyed a hay-day of overt resurgence since the U.S. presidential election in 2016, and it seems loathe to crawl back under the hoods and into the shadows of yesteryear, much less loose its (hopefully dying) grasp on the modern American psyche, and the world. Its virulent vehemence poses a frightening threat to the project of American democracy and to anyone who stands for the ideals of equality and justice, particularly for women, femmes, trans, and Black, Brown, and Indigenous people of color.

Even prior to the official election day in 2020, voter turnout was unprecedented, with lines of prospective voters snaking around city blocks and bearing hours-long wait times in all manner of weather during a deadly pandemic, all for their chance to have their voice counted on one side or the other of this seemingly

---

[27] See Richardson, Heather Cox. *How the South Won the Civil War: Oligarchy, Democracy, and the Continuing Fight for the Soul of America.* Oxford University Press: New York, NY, 2020.

interminable fight. *Who will win? Who will lose?* The whole country, it seems—and indeed, the world—gets drawn in with bated breath, riveted to the unfolding the drama of power.

But we are asking the wrong question, and in so doing contemporaneously upholding a paradigm that does not serve us: that of a dialectic of winning versus losing, of an "us" versus "them" binary opposition. This sets up a false dichotomy predicated on social division and antagonism. Preoccupation with such a narrative keeps us separate and distracted from the possibility of organizing together to build social systems that really *do* serve us. But rather than exiting the Colosseum, or better yet tearing it down altogether, we stay in the stands cheering either for the lion or the warrior, glued to the spectacle of bloodshed.

This has been the prevailing paradigm for the last several thousand years, and it has caused generations upon generations of collective trauma from violence, death, and grief. This is the legacy that we bear as the human species, and we have been keeping score for millennia with no end in sight. The only thing that has changed is the technology and sophistication of our apparatuses of war—who has more and bigger armies, guns, or bombs—with which to terrify and terrorize one's opponents into submission.

We have weaponry now with the capacity to end all life on earth many times over. Is that enough? We are all, collectively, held hostage at the end of the barrel of our own fanatical fear, hatred, and willingness to other and condemn. We are thus stuck on this not-so-merry-go-round of fear and hate, and fear and hate, breeding only more fear and hate... But it is a trick and a trap

101

based on the delusion of our separateness, a false-flag narrative of winners and losers—us versus them. There is no such thing as "other," just as there is no such thing as winning or losing. Because in truth, either all of us win or none of us do.

This is the paradigm of colonization, which we have inherited for generations upon generations, since the first dawning of modern "civilizations" created societies based on *subjugational*[28] hierarchy, which the West has succeeded in disseminating wholesale across the globe through the apparatus of violent imperialism. Our societies, our relationships to one another, and even to our own selves, have been shaped by this myth of superiority and inferiority, of winners and losers, of "us" versus "them." Such a colonized worldview sabotages our ability to be in organic, authentic, and intimate connection with those with whom we share this world—because we are constantly calculating our relative positions within intersecting[29] hierarchies of race, class, gender, sexuality, ability, size, looks, and whatever other cultural codes are used to determine ones value, acceptance, belonging, and power within a group or society—and it undermines our own deepest internal sense of self-worth, empowerment, and vitality.

I call this internal colonizer the "Inner Fascist." The Inner Fascist not only upholds and projects imperialist narratives of

---

[28]I distinguish here between *functional* hierarchies, which exist temporarily for a specific purpose and need not treat people as more or less worthy, versus *subjugational* hierarchy which do treat people as more or less worthy and attempt to maintain this prejudicial and oppressive structure as part of an enduring status quo.

[29] Thanks to Black writer and activist Kimberlé Crenshaw for the articulation of the concept of *intersectionality*.

superiority and inferiority onto other people and the world through the prejudices of racism, sexism and chauvinism, classism, ageism, ableism, xenophobia, homophobia, transphobia, and/or fatphobia, but perhaps even more insidiously it has us perpetrate these abuses *upon ourselves*.

As with social fascisms, the Inner Fascist measures and compares our value and inherent worth according to the arbitrary and superficial "faults" or "triumphs" of others. If we are perceived to be smarter, prettier, thinner, whiter, richer, stronger, more masculine, more heteronormative, more principled or self-righteous, then we judge ourselves as better than those who aren't. On the flip side, if we perceive ourselves to be less smart, less pretty, fatter, darker, poorer, weaker, more femme, less heteronormative, or subject to foibles of character, then we judge ourselves to be less worthy—and this judgment is confirmed and perpetuated by the social status quo. But such a stark binary does not allow either us or others to be fully authentic and multidimensional expressions of our unique human selves, with all our myriad qualities and challenges which not only make us who we are, but which are the divine expression of the unfurling universe[30] in the form of us. When we don't allow ourselves to be *who we are*, we deny the sacred mandate of our life and rob the collective of the benefit of our unique genius.

Furthermore, the Inner Fascist keeps us dependent and in fear for our security and continued existence. We live in fear that we will be harmed—that our emotional or physical boundaries will

---

[30] Thanks to Brian Swimme for this terminology; see *The Universe Story*, Harper Collins: San Francisco, 1992.

be violated by others, that we will be forced to submit to the will of another, that we will lose control over our own lives and circumstances, or that we will be abandoned and left alone, vulnerable, and unloved, ostracized from our community or from society, left to fend for ourselves or starve and die in the wilderness.

This may sound bleak and hyperbolic, but these fears have a deep biological and psychological lineage within us, not only from the times when our ancient ancestors' physical security and continued existence in nature depended on their belonging to a group or tribe, but from our own infancy and early childhood when our physical survival and emotional wellbeing depended on our connection to and validation from our parental units and immediate family. In the perceived absence of these very necessary protections and validation of our emotional and physical security, the Inner Fascist steps in as a force of control and stability to defend against any possible threats to our continued existence. And without a regular and robust external source for such emotional and physical support, we come to rely on the defensive protection of the Inner Fascist first and foremost throughout our lives.

The Inner Fascist is the proverbial strongman. A dictator, an oppressor, a tyrant. We resort to submitting to a strongman ideology—and to those who play the strongman role in the world—believing that this strongman, this Inner (or outer) Fascist, will save us, rather than accepting the power and responsibility of our own self-agency.

The terrible irony is that the protection of the Inner Fascist is not zero-sum but comes with the cost of our own freedom. We find ourselves walled-in by our own defensive posturing at the behest of the Inner Fascist and within the coercive confines of our self-protection we find that *we* become our own greatest adversary.

By subjugating ourselves to the fears and protective defenses of the Inner Fascist we inevitably isolate ourselves from the very sense of belonging and connection that we crave. In order to avoid the painful threat of abandonment and ostracism, we unwittingly cut ourselves off from engaging in authentic and vulnerable intimacy. The Inner Fascist tells us that love is conditional, that we have to be good enough to deserve love and connection, and that because we are inescapably an inherently flawed human being, we can never be good enough to deserve to be loved the way we want and need to be. This belief creates a self-fulfilling prophesy in which we denigrate ourselves, hold ourselves apart from others, and try to shut down the vital living force within us that does in fact need and deserve unconditional love and acceptance. Worse still, because of our perceived inherent wretchedness we cannot even consent to love ourselves, and so *we* reject and abandon *ourselves*, which only serves to prove to us that we are, indeed, unlovable.

Meanwhile, in order to maintain a sense of control over our lives and circumstances, we perhaps inadvertently coerce and attempt to subjugate those around us as well as force ourselves, our own creative expressive vitality, into rigidly defined confines of what is considered to be strong, powerful, attractive, and therefore acceptable. From this perspective we feel that any affront to or diversion from our own definition of what constitutes right thought or action is a challenge and a threat to our "okayness" in the world, and that to yield to such a challenge or threat would not only be a sign of weakness, but will lead to the collapse of our carefully orchestrated existence. Moreover, since our experience of the world, of reality, according to the Inner Fascist, is dependent on our *rightness*, if we allow for the possibility that the world may not be *exactly* as we ordain it to be, then that must inevitably mean that all of society and the world as we know it is also not okay and not safe.

This is the definition of cognitive dissonance and it is here that we find that the reality constructed by the Inner Fascist is like a Jenga tower of judgements—of others and of oneself—and that in order to keep it standing, and thereby secure one's own sense of rightness, virtue, and superiority—or self-*righteousness*—one must live up to each and every fragile, precarious judgmental brick. For each one that gets proven faulty, the whole tower of one's sense of power and control, of right and wrong, threatens to come crashing down, and with it one's sense of goodness, of value, and of power and security in the world.

Once again, we find that the Inner Fascist spins a narrative of conditional worth, convincing us that we must prove our value above and against that of others, and that if we fail to do so we become powerless victims. Because in a dialectic of right and wrong, winners and losers, superiority and inferiority, if you're not one then by necessity you must be the other. If you're not right then you must be wrong; if you're not winning then you must be losing; if you're not superior then you're bound to be violated at the wills and whims of those who are. Therefore, you must exert your rightness and superiority at every turn and at all costs.

But the cost, of course, is who you truly are, or would be, if you would only let yourself be in the full, authentic, spontaneous, and free expression of your humanity. Instead, you whip and castigate yourself into playing a role, into asserting a perpetually fragile superiority over and above not only others, but your own true self. And thus, in a tragic turn of events, it is you who violates the boundaries of your own integrity.

108

CHAPTER FIFTEEN

CHANGE AND THE SPIRITUAL LEFT

STANDPOINT

At the opposing pole of contemporary worldviews held by the Religious Right stands the Spiritual Left. Its relationship to the Political Left is analogous to, but more poorly defined than, that between the Religious Right and Political Right. The principal difference between those two poles lies in the way history is— or is not—used to command allegiance.

HISTORY

Those who remember history are doomed to repeat it.

What a miserable story of exploitation and suffering human history is: an endless litany of wrongs and revenges, hatreds and guilts, victims and perpetrators. Our inability to forget the past keeps it alive, an oozing wound that never has the chance to heal. Like a ship dragging its anchor, we do not sail into the future because we do not jettison our collective history of enmity.

We go to extraordinary lengths to remember past glories (the "conquest" of other peoples and the wilds of nature) and humiliations (other people's past glories at our expense). It isn't just public education that keeps regurgitating past history, of course—it's politicians and military strategists and their disinformation arm, corporate media. Conflicts, hatreds, wrongs: There is no offensive act that cannot be justified by the past.

We refuse to forget history and so we keep repeating it.

Things do not change and that is what conservatives want. That is what *conservative* means. *Hold on to the past. Resist change. Return to the past.*

While some factions of monotheistic religions promote progressive and liberal ideals, most find that the conservative nature of their dogma aligns with the objectives of the Political Right. The marriage of the Religious Right and the Political Right is not confined to the U.S. culture war, of course—and we do not have to look hard to see just how facilely that marriage gives birth to theocracy, authoritarianism, totalitarianism, and fascism.

THE SPIRITUAL LEFT

The Spiritual Left is the complement of the Religious Right. The other half of the human psyche. The half grounded in a trust of life rather than a fear of it.

It is progressive, in the sense that it seeks out positive change, seeks to move on, seeks a better vision. It is liberal, in the sense that it accepts differences, embraces differences, finds the sameness within differences. It is progressive and liberal in the sense that it is not restrained by the past: it does not simply forget the past—it forgives and it seeks forgiveness.

It is, however, first and foremost, a spiritual lifeway.

Lifeways that identify as *spiritual* rather than traditionally *religious* tend to focus on the present. A spiritual practice often entails cultivating sincere goodwill toward all and a consistent "mindful" awareness of the present moment. Despite its ancient roots in indigenous animistic worldviews, it is a curiously modern perspective in the sense of living consciously within the relativity of an Einsteinian universe (in which there is no objective past-present-future) and the instantaneity of a quantum-entangled universe (in which information passes instantly, unconstrained by distance). Both ancient and modern, this spiritual practice of *living-in-the-present* involves an authentic relinquishing of cognitive-emotional attachments to the past, as well as hopes, fears, and expectations of the future. It is a positive disinterestedness in the fallacies of memory and projection in favor of the living present.

However, *the present moment* does not mean just attending to the ever-flowing stream of "news" generated by corporate and social media.

Such one-sided focus on the completely ephemeral and skewed opinions of professionals and nonprofessionals alike subsumes all the other, more essential facets of our present experience of the universe.

The present moment is the totality of raw experience, unfiltered by our internal running commentary on experience. It encompasses the totality of internal and external experiences stemming from our interactions with culture and nature. A spiritual lifeway leads to contentment precisely because it calls us to disengage from the social conditioning which, like gravity, pulls us back toward groupthink and away from our natural state of buoyant free-thinking individuality.

Likewise, *wisdom* does not mean forgetting the *lessons* humanity has gleaned from its collective past—rather, it means *not fetishizing* past experiences.

At its best, the Spiritual Left embodies wisdom and compassion. Not the rote wisdom of dogma, but the creative and adaptive response of intuitive intelligence to changing circumstances—a kind of wisdom that subordinates self-interest to the greatest good and deals with the long-range consequences of actions ahead of time. Nor is it the golden rule receiving little more than lip service on Sunday, but the compassion of deep-seated identification with the sacredness of humanity and nature without exception.

The alignment of the *Spiritual Left* and the *Political Left* is a natural alliance, since they share many of the same values of egalitarianism and peaceful coexistence. But it is also a tenuous one, since the Political Left has become embroiled in a power struggle with the Political Right that runs counter to the deepest values of the Spiritual Left.

The Political Left, in other words, has taken the bait of the Political Right and entered into an antagonistic relationship that has polarized a nation into political paralysis.

In a highly-charged polarized environment, what does venting anger and outright rejection of the other side accomplish but to reinforce their own righteous indignation and the sense that their way of life is under attack? Certainly, this is the effect of the

Left's words and actions upon the Right—but it is no less so the effect of the Right's words and actions upon the Left.

Both sides dig in deeper, in a kind of mental trench warfare, lobbing word bombs and political strategies at one another in the vain belief that victory will soon be won. It is a war of scoring points, as if the other side will finally be convinced either by superior reasoning or by votes.

The U.S. has become the Indig-Nation: everything the Right does stirs righteous indignation in the Left, everything the Left does stirs righteous indignation in the Right. From the standpoint of the Spiritual Left, the strategy of the Political Left is not working—it simply contributes to the ongoing polarization of the citizenry while the real opponents, the ruling oligarchy, continue to dictate the direction of civilization from the shadows.

Wisdom considers it axiomatic that everyone acts for the sake of what they believe to be good.

Within a political context, this presents as the basis of compassion and empathy. Even with those we oppose ideologically, we can be moved to understand their perspective and make the effort to move them to the center. At the very least, we can avoid retreating into sophisticated cynicism and clever irony as a means of ridiculing others' positions. A moderate position to adopt is to recognize that others are sincere in the pursuit of their beliefs and so, to *neither take offense nor give offense.*

Self-criticism is an essential part of wisdom, one that brings our respective shortcomings into sharp relief. This is especially valuable when reflecting on the relationship between the Spiritual Left and the Political Left and the way they mutually strengthen one another: *Just as the Spiritual Left learns from the Political Left that it must not withdraw from the world of action, the Political Left learns from the Spiritual Left that it must not right wrongs by committing wrongs.*

Once we have adopted the tactics of the Right, we have ceded the moral high ground. And without the moral high ground, minds cannot be changed nor can hearts be won.

CHANGE

Take for example the concept of *The Turning Point: At the Pinnacle of Waxing, the Inevitable Waning Begins.* This is a lesson—not the memory of a specific historical event—that encompasses a wide swath of human experience, grounded in recognizable cycles of natural phenomena. *Once something has reached the limits of its growth, it needs to contract back onto itself in order to consolidate its resources in preparation for the next cycle of growth.*

It is a lesson embodying the famous saying by Giuseppe Tomasi di Lampedusa in his novel *The Leopard*: "If we want things to stay the same, everything will have to change." If we want to continue to have anything like the kind of life we have now, we will need to make fundamental system-wide adaptations to a world of escalating social and environmental change. It is, of course, upon this point that the Right and Left must ultimately build consensus.

114

Political strategies running contrary to wisdom, on the other hand, arrogantly seek to expand a nation's influence forever. With the inevitable result of depleting its energy, resources and national will. In place of a measured strategic contraction, such tactics precipitate a fall from the very power they sought to seize and hold. Anyone advocating for continued expansion of influence, power, or environmental exploitation in this time is blind to the writing on the wall.

Moving beyond history allows us to encounter change in our own time—and when has such a confluence of profound technological, environmental, and social changes ever converged as they do now? We live in a time without precedent and we know it. No generation before us has faced such a perfect storm of change.

What especially distinguishes this from other times is that we ourselves are making decisions that can either escalate these global problems or defuse them. Paradoxically, we as individuals are empowering ourselves by making constructive decisions even as our social institutions continue exacerbating the problems, contributing to our underlying sense of powerlessness. This disconnect between the citizenry and their rulers has become a symptom of failed nation-states and one that any self-aware ruling body corrects without hesitation.

Encountering change means not getting distracted by contrived issues. It entails seeing through the hype of corporate and social media and into the heart of those problems of the first magnitude, those problems affecting humanity itself. There is no other way to draw people together and move into a present marked by collaboration and cooperation. Other peoples cannot

115

trust our motives until we consistently demonstrate a selflessness of purpose—one that strives for peace and prospering for all people everywhere, absent any advantage for ourselves.

Encountering change means looking at why things aren't changing for the better. Purely political solutions that fail to incorporate wisdom and compassion don't change things because they are aimed at the wrong target. It takes both wisdom and compassion to reach the inevitable goal of universal amnesty and reconciliation. Any other goal is secondary, as it requires a unified citizenry to establish a viable civilization for hundreds of generations to come. Is there really any other goal worthy of our lives and deaths?

Feet, what do I need you for when I have wings to fly?
~ Frida Kahlo

This quote of Frida Kahlo perfectly captures the spirit of the Spiritual Left, which holds that the mundane issues will resolve themselves once the universal issues have been resolved. It is the power of imagination—not reason or memory—that gives the human psyche flight, allowing it to discover unsuspected and unforeseen solutions to long-standing problems. It is in the landscape of the imagination, as well, that people of all cultures and all times meet on the common ground of art, music, and philosophy.

SUM

Encountering change is not dissimilar to staring wide-eyed into a gale-force wind. It is seldom comfortable, causing as it does the stress of uncertainty and insecurity. It can blur our vision,

116

causing us to see things that aren't there even as it causes us to miss things that are. But change *is* the present moment. It never occurs in the past or future. It is where our full attention needs to dwell if we are to maintain that unique ability to adapt readily to extraordinary circumstances which made our most ancient ancestors the species of such extraordinary potential that it did.

118

Chapter Sixteen

The Waterslide

I want to tell you a story.

It's a story about a trip down a waterslide.

It was mid-August 2018, what seems an eternity ago, back when we could still take so many things for granted.

It was my friend Shockie's 34th birthday. I met Shockie and her wife, Bombshell, through roller derby, and hence we always refer to each other by our "derby names." For her birthday Shockie had invited a group of us—myself, Scratch, Scratch's girlfriend Eileen, Tricki, Ziggy, and of course Bombshell—to rent tubes and go floating down a nearby river. I tend not to be someone who "does things," per se. I'm more of a homebody— which is just another way of saying that I'm straight-up boring, which is the truth—but I had recently made up my mind to make more of an effort to nurture my friendships, especially with good, wholesome, creative, fun, and sincere people like the Shocks (as we called them), and I wanted to support and celebrate my friend on her birthday. So, with images of basking belly-up in the open sunshine, the cool fresh water tickling our toes, and with perhaps a drink in hand, I anticipated a pleasant afternoon in good company.

Then, on the morning of our special birthday outing the skies opened up with a deluge of rain and the threat of lightening which dashed our lazy dreams. I was sincerely disappointed, and we tried to brainstorm alternative ideas for possible indoor shenanigans. That's when Shockie (to my utmost chagrin) elected that we should all go to the nearby indoor water park. (Yikes, I thought. I mean, WHAT FUN!)

Now, normally I wouldn't be caught dead at a waterpark, indoor or otherwise. The very thought of it sets me on edge—all those people gathered in close proximity, everything damp, the pungent acrid smell of chlorine hanging in the air and slimy wet children screaming and running amok. No, thank you. But I wanted to make the effort to play nicely with others, make friends, and not be a spoilsport, so I set my trepidations aside, grabbed my bathing suit, and hopped in the car.

It was more or less exactly (as bad) as I had imagined. Entering the park was like running smack into a wall of hot, moist, sticky, vaporized chlorine. My lungs protested and my heart began to pound in panic as I gulped for fresh air (in vain). I tried to remind myself that if no one else was suffocating in here then neither would I and to just calm down and relax. (What fun!).

The high glass walls echoed with the shrieks of children, running from pool to pool, their wet feet slapping on the warm, glistening concrete. I surveyed the chaos dubiously, perhaps as Dante might some circle of hell. There were various different pools and features—a small kiddie pool where grandparents and new moms sat with their young toddlers splashing innocuously; a large wave pool with a simulated waterfall feature where children and adults in innertubes rocked languidly on the puny

120

waves; a pool with low basketball hoops; a large faux-tropical wooden structure that would periodically dump a load of water on the gaggles of children climbing and playing on its scaffolding (I made a mental note to steer clear of that area); and several waterslides of different colors, a dinky light blue one, labeled "Category 1," that was clearly for babies, and two larger twisty slides, yellow and red—Categories 2 and 3, respectively—for the bigger kids.

My group of middle-aged friends and I found a table where we could park our towels and bags before changing into our bathing suits and courageously—if a bit self-consciously, for our age—entered the fray.

The wave-pool was pleasant enough—disconcertingly lukewarm, and tame—but crowded and, quite frankly, boring. Before long one of my friends suggested we pick things up a bit by trying the slides and we all eagerly acquiesced, tramping over to the stairs leading up to the entrance to the twisty tubes. Upon reaching the first landing, however, I noticed a sign tacked next to the red and yellow slides that read, "only those under 120lbs allowed," and I realized with slight chagrin that these slides were strictly for children and that I had not fit into this particular category for quite some time. It was at this point that it began to dawn on me that perhaps I was getting myself into more than I had bargained for.

But there was no turning back now. This is what one does at an indoor waterpark and I was trying to be a team player and go with the flow—to turn back now would have been just so square and boring, and too typical of an old me, a more anxious and inhibited me. So, on up I went, dutifully plodding after my

121

friends, a grown-ass woman scared to go down a silly waterslide, but even more scared to admit that she was faking it, desperately, this act of free-wheeling confidence. (…What fun…)

At the top of the staircase we arrived at a platform with two large holes in the wall, one colored dark green and large enough around to fit an adult human, and one orange and slightly larger to accommodate an innertube. These were labeled Category 4 and 5, respectively. The slides that I had anticipated riding were the ones for children whose twists and turns I could see and appraise for myself. But alas, those were not for me. These slides went outside the building, their contortions a mystery, before depositing their riders back inside the park into a pool two-stories below.

Standing between these two gaping holes stood the obligatory bored teenager, half-heartedly monitoring the slide-goers as they, one by one, got into position at the mouths of these menacing maws before disappearing with echoes of hooting glee into the unseen bowels.

Holding in mind the corresponding categories assigned to hurricanes, and given that I did not have an innertube, I chose the line for the lower and less ominously categorized green slide. Scratchy, Eileen, Bombshell, and Tricki had all carried innertubes with them, so they dispatched to the Category 5, while I queued up behind Shockie and Ziggy.

Shockie disappeared first with a howl, arms flown above her head in wild abandon.

Ziggy followed without trepidation in a perhaps more sensible corpse pose, arms crossed tightly over her chest.

Now I was the last one left standing on the platform and, without thinking too much about what I was about to do, slid my legs into that hollow maw. My hands gripped the edges of the wet plastic as I waited for the indifferent teenager to give me the go-ahead. But he was distracted by a group of kids clamoring on inner tubes next to me, eager to push off into the exhilarating plunge.

What if I went too soon? Would I run into Ziggy in the middle of the tube? Or come splashing out on top of her at the bottom? But surely it's been long enough, I thought. If I waited any longer I might lose my nerve! And with that thought I steeled myself and took my hands away from the edges of the tube, leaned back, scooching my butt further down the slippery plastic, and began to slide irreversibly forward.

Inside the tube was pitch black, the dark green plastic emitting absolutely no light from the outside. I stared blankly into the darkness as I plunged with increasing speed, the only sensation the cool slippery water at my back, lubricating my descent, and the bump, bump, bump of the junction seams of the hard plastic sections of tube rhythmically knocking against the back of my head as I went, progressively faster and faster, turning this way and now jerking that way. It didn't take long—a few seconds at most—for me to realize that I had made a horrible mistake, as my body was whipped from side to side, and then upside down in a loop-dee-loop, losing all sense of direction and spatial relation. I was twisting, spinning, shooting through sheer darkness with nothing but my breath to rely on.

"Just breathe," I reminded myself.

I tried to take deep steady breaths through my nose, despite the jerking and jostling—my mouth, jaw, and eyes all clamped shut, every muscle in my body taut with fear. The air entering and exiting my lungs was my only comfort and I leaned into it as a lifeline. "As long as you're breathing," I thought, "you know you're not dying," as my stomach lurched around another curve, through another upside-down loop, my limbs lost for a sense of gravity, for anything to grab hold of.

There was no stopping this. And no telling how long this groundless chaos would last. Rationally I knew it couldn't go on forever, but still, in the heart of the uncontrollable twisting darkness, a deeply subliminal part of me still wondered: "what if this *is* forever?" And in that moment it might as well have been. In such a moment of terror and utter helplessness it almost doesn't matter that or if or when it might end. Because all that matters in that moment is that what is happening cannot be stopped.

And in that moment, which stretches on for what might as well be an eternity, when I realized with gut-wrenching terror that the solid ground which I had always taken for granted was no longer there beneath my feet, I found a kind of secret doorway, a threshold, within myself. On the one side was the terror of this seemingly endless descent, this unraveling of everything I thought was stable and dependable about the world, and which crushed my chest in an icy panic; and on the other side was, perhaps paradoxically, a kind of freedom.

124

Between these two sides, I found, swings a door bearing that much maligned term: "Acceptance." Or maybe it's "Surrender," which isn't any better, with its connotations of powerlessness in defeat. We like to think that we are in control—of our minds, of our bodies, of our lives (and perhaps even those of others)—such that to accept or surrender is to admit our submission and our powerlessness in the face of reality—of what, simply, is.

"But no! I must be *free!*" we exclaim. "*I* must be able to choose that which befalls me, *my* fate, *my* destiny!" And yet, here I am, half-naked shooting every-which-way through a pitch-dark tube with no recourse to stop it or choose any alternative to the current situation. (What fun.)

I felt the panic rise up in my chest like bile—

"Wait," I thought, "*is* it bile? No, it's panic. It's definitely panic. (Oh thank god it's just panic!)"

—as I clenched my entire body against this inescapable ordeal. "Just breathe," I reminded myself again.

And there it was again, that door! With each steady, measured breath—as I career through this twisting netherworld—the door swings open and I glimpse what is there on the other side of this infernal ordeal. With each breath I can feel myself coming back to myself. Despite the panic I must not run away, must not abandon myself in this, my hour of need.

No, the running, the resistance to the terror itself only serves to feed the terror. My desire—no matter how true, no matter how justified, no matter how righteous—to make it stop, to rewind, to go back to the top, to the beginning, and make a different choice—in other words my *insistence* on control, on exercising *my free will*, dammit!—*is* the very torment of my current circumstance. And it will not have its way (except with me) so long as I feed it my fear.

Oh, the irony that my grasping for ultimate freedom should become instead this torment of fate, tossing me about like a ragdoll in the jaws of a Rottweiler, a turmoil of my own making to rival that of the tube! The irony that my need for freedom from my circumstance should hold me captive to it, while freedom should be found in the surrender to my fate, to what I cannot control.

But for the breath, that familiar touchstone, swinging wide the door of surrender and acceptance to the truth and totality of the moment, I might have lost myself to the panic of that swirling vortex, whether of my own mind or the tube, I can hardly tell.

And then there it was, a light! The literal light at the end of the tunnel came rushing towards, engulfed me, and, before I knew it, I shot out of the end of the tunnel and was instantly submerged. Blinking blearily through the stinging chlorine haze I could see nothing but bubbles and froth all around me. For one terrible moment I had no idea which way was up and frantically reminded myself that I don't have to know, I only have to hold my breath until I float to the surface.

I came up sputtering and shaking. The first thing I saw was Shockie's face beaming back at me with the ecstatic, stricken look of one who has just survived rites, a kind of baptism by fire—or water, as it were. I swam clumsily towards her, as one scrabbles towards a port in a storm. *Land, ho!* The world had righted itself once more—I could tell up from down, I hadn't died, and soon I had my feet firmly back on solid concrete. I shakily hauled myself out of the pool and, on adrenaline-induced Bambi legs, tottered back to our table where I slumped gratefully into a chair and, still breathing heavily, took stock of what I'd just experienced.

~

I immediately recognized my trip down the waterslide as an almost religious awakening, or at the very least a profound metaphor for the uncontrollability of life…and death.

We are all on the waterslide. We are all in this erratic unpredictable, sometimes tortuous (and torturous), often serpentine conveyance called Life. We all suffer our own personal waterslides when our lives are turned upside down— the loss of a loved one, an illness, or other crisis of the soul; and we also struggle through collective waterslides—poverty and economic inequality, the rise of anti-democratic fascism and extremist factions, the fear of social and ecological collapse, and pandemics as well. I think most would agree that at this moment in history (which certainly goes beyond even the writing of this in 2020), it often seems that the tunnel is getting darker, the pace swifter, the turns sharper. We are continually wrenched by whiplash from one seeming catastrophe to the next—from one political corruption scandal to the next, from one police murder to the next, from one natural disaster to the next, from one more calamitous study on the effects of climate change to the next, from one social uprising to the next—without time for our hearts to mend, or our minds to get a grips and regain our equilibrium.

For many of those of us in the United States, we perhaps first felt this slippery slope on the morning of November 9th, 2016, when we woke up to the fact that not only did a large faction of our populace willfully support forces of vocal white supremacist fascism, but that the very democratic process and ideal of majority rule, which is the foundation of our government, has been woefully corrupted. Since that day we in the U.S. have watched as blatant white supremacists and self-proclaimed neo-Nazis have marched through our city streets; as voting in predominantly urban, Black, democratic, and low-income communities has been significantly restricted; as environmental protections have been tossed aside in favor of wanton exploitation of natural resources for corporate profit; as the rich have been allowed to grow exponentially richer to a level unprecedented in history and so obscene it is literally inconceivable to the human intellect; as the majority of citizens, who struggle to maintain even the most basic standard of existence (I will not deign to call it "living") are pushed ever closer to, and often passed, the brink of bankruptcy and houselessness; as Black, Indigenous, and peoples of color continue to be wantonly and unceremoniously brutalized, gunned down, suffocated, and enslaved—yes, enslaved, according to the 13th Amendment of the US Constitution—by the foot soldiers of our—and *their*—own government; as South and Central American refugees are illegally imprisoned and tortured; as suicide rates continue to rise across demographics of age, race, and gender; as we battle compounding epidemics of income inequality, health care disparities, and opioid addiction; and now, as a global pandemic has been let run rampant through our country, largely unchecked, and only exacerbating and rendering bare the systemic injustices that already plagued this supposedly great nation.

To be fair, these realities are not necessarily a direct result of the outcome of the 2016 presidential election—most of them, with the exception of the Covid-19 pandemic, have existed to varying degrees, often under a shroud of secrecy and/or willful denial, for centuries. Certainly, the forty-fifth president of the United States did not invent the systems of imperialist white supremacist capitalist cisheteropatriarchy—which have existed since well before the founding of this country and are embedded in its history and political apparatuses. But the consequences of these systems of injustice have all grown demonstrably worse over the past several decades—concurrent with the neoliberal stronghold of Congress, the presidency, and federal policies— and have either gotten exponentially worse in the last several years or have failed to be mitigated in any substantive way. The result, or perhaps the intent, of all this—rendered particularly acute by the willful inaction of the U.S. government response to the Covid-19 pandemic crisis—seems to be a rather bald-faced objective by those elites in power to simply let "the masses" die or kill each other off, whether by illness and disease, poverty, or violent factionalism along racial and political lines. Meanwhile the wealth and resources needed to survive in this "civilization" continue to be amassed by a privileged few who seem to think that their money will protect them from the impending collapse.

This is, of course, nothing but a fool's paradise, as there will be no survival on a dead planet (which includes Mars, by the way), and true wealth has always been measured not in hoarded resources but in robust relationships of community solidarity. The joke's on them…I guess.

Thus far I have focused on the story of the United States, though many of the themes elucidated above run rampant through many if not most countries, as well as the corporate stronghold on business and industry world-wide. The more recent descent of U.S. politics and society into an experience of near-apocalyptic loss of normalcy and control has been jarring to many (particularly white, middle-class or affluent) Americans, but many peoples the world over have already been experiencing these crises for a long time yet.

Across the globe the vast majority of the world's population has been kept in extreme poverty, left vulnerable to disease, starvation, and various forms of modern slavery. Many have been forced to flee their homes, their lands, or their countries, due to the ramifications of the often compounding forces of colonialism, dictatorial fascism, civil and international wars, and climate disruption. These people have already lost or been forced to leave behind any semblance of normalcy, comfort, familiarity, or control over their circumstances, instead taking the risk of finding new communities, new opportunity, and new life in foreign countries amongst strangers in unfamiliar cultures. Those who do find homes elsewhere often face virulent racism, ostracism, and violence, while those who don't end up foundering in barely survivable, inhumane refugee camps—that is, of course, if they survive the migrant passage at all.

Each of these stories is a trauma. We feel ourselves—and our world—slipping, losing our grip on the familiar, on what once seemed stable and constant, predictable, controllable. We find ourselves collectively falling, plummeting to an unknown end by some unknown and rapidly changing trajectory. We are all on this waterslide, together, with no indication of how or when it will end.

~

The waterslide, this experience of a dark plummeting groundlessness, is what some might call *fate*. It is what is; that which we, puny humans, have no recourse to stop or change. The terror induced by such an experience grips us at our very core and sends us into psychic spasms of panic and resistance. We clamor for some relief, some exit, any way to be free of the torment of living in such a violent and unjust world.

In our struggle to get away from this reality, from the simple, inescapable totality of what is, we often end up carelessly abandoning ourselves—furiously repressing or contemptuously turning away from our own sensitive hearts stricken with terror, grief, and rage—as we rail against our own impotence in the face of untenable circumstances. We feel utterly powerless, trapped, like a wounded animal, a hopeless victim of a cruel world.

And yes, perhaps there is some truth in this. No one of us has the power to change any of the litany of injustices and abuses that we encounter in this world, or in life in general, much less that ultimate injustice—the fact that all things die, that every sacred event, every unique being, every novel creation of the universe, will inevitably be irrevocably lost.

This is, of course, the ultimate symbolic significance of the waterslide as an allegory for the uncontrollable inevitability of death, of the loss of that which cannot be replaced. Which is also what perpetually breaks our hearts and inflames our senses with rage when we witness lives and Life so recklessly, callously, and casually treated as expendable. It is unconscionable. And yet, here we are, naked and afraid, plunging through this wretched nightmare with no recourse to stop it. (And no, it is no fucking fun.)

It is true—we cannot resist the often cruel hand of fate, and doing so often risks doing more harm than good, as we thrash against our constraints. In truth it is that very resistance to circumstance, to *what is* in any given moment, that exacerbates our torment into a frenzy of panic and powerlessness—it is the desire, the need, to make it stop that turns the ride of Life into some sort of torture device, and thereby confirms our victimhood; or, in other words, "seals our fate."

And from this position, from this perspective, we *are* powerless. But that is not the only truth. Because we always have within us the freedom to choose how we respond to circumstances, to fate, to the world, and Life, as it is. But such a choice is never a done-deal, because it must be constantly made afresh in each new and ever-changing moment. Such choice, such freedom, requires one bring a core of and commitment to *integrity*—which is the very opposite of reactionary compulsion—as well as *conscientious self-awareness* to every thought and action.

And it requires that one *accept* and *surrender* to what is, to fate. Resistance breeds resistance; war breeds war. Acceptance and integrity allow for action imbued with sincere *intention*, rather than simply rote or compulsive *re*action. Moreover, surrender is an act of *faith*. It is not only an acknowledgment but a co-creative conception of (and with) the divine in everything. In surrender we not only find ourselves held in the sacred embrace

132

of divinity, but we are responsible for embodying and manifesting that divinity as immanent to the living world.

This is crucial. It is a vital and reciprocal, co-creative, collaborative way of re-ensouling an enchanted world and cosmos, as well as of envisioning a new mode of existence on this planet. In truth, our cosmos has always been and remains immanently enchanted—as ancient and indigenous wisdom traditions teach us—but it has become *dis-enchanted* within the dualistic materialism of the modern Western, imperialist white supremacist capitalist cisheteropatriarchal worldview.

We cannot continue doing things the old way, the way that has sought to divide and conquer, exploit and exterminate, leaving us broken, broken-hearted, and enraged. We cannot dismantle the master's house using the master's tools. We must envision and have the courage to respond in radically new ways to the crises we face.

Instead of grasping for equilibrium in a broken system and world, we must have the courage to stay in disequilibrium, to let ourselves fall and perhaps fall apart, to embrace the collapse of all we knew and relied upon before, and instead lean into the faith that there is something more than this, something bigger than us puny humans with our catalogue of mistakes, and possibly even something greater to come.

This is not to say that the fear, pain, and loss that come with the fall are not real, are not devastating, are not significant. They are. And what—or who—may be lost in the process is inviolably imbued with immeasurable worth, and thus cannot be replaced. Rather than resist the inevitability of such losses, rather than deny or ignore, repress or evade the agonizing reality of suffering, uncertainty, and, yes, even death, there is always the possibility of not just finding but *creating* another doorway, another way of relating—from our own sensitive hearts ringing with love, courage, and hope—to this thing called Life.

And then, when the light at the end of the tunnel finally comes, we will not come sputtering up from the depths only to find more of the same—it will not be the violent, broken world we left behind. We will instead have created a portal and crossed a threshold into a new world and a new way of living in it—with ourselves and with one another—which is no longer predicated on insecurity and fear, division and competition, scarcity and exploitation, violence and cruelty, but on integrity and faith, trust and solidarity, compassion, forgiveness, and *Belonging*.

We will still—always—be on the waterslide, but no longer will we feel powerless to fate; rather, we will know not only our own resilience and capacity for acceptance and surrender in the face of circumstances outside our control, but we will also be able to find joy in the exhilaration of the ride.

CHAPTER SEVENTEEN

CHILDREN'S SUFFRAGE

Every child from the age of six years has the right to vote.

Any argument you can make against this ideal can be made against half the adults who have the right to vote.

Of course, the voting age will be lowered by degrees, first to twelve or ten, before finally settling on age six.

This will be the single greatest change to democracy in history.

CHAPTER EIGHTEEN

SPIRITUAL ANARCHY OR THE INNER FASCIST

PART II

In order to keep ourselves safe from violation, subjugation, and ultimately annihilation under perceived threats in the external world, we keep ourselves locked away and deprived of a full, free, and emotionally and physically nourishing existence. Pain and suffering, grief and death, are undeniable parts of life. But as much as they are unavoidable they are also utterly unbearable. When in the exquisite grips of acute pain, grief, or psychospiritual suffering, we feel that it is untenable, that we cannot go on, that we will be annihilated by it. We flail and grope for any means to escape such physical and emotional torment—rigid denial of what is happening, pure blind rage at the injustice, pathetic bargaining for any respite—or else we sink into a paralytic despair, bereft of any hope to change our lot.

Here the Inner Fascist has little to do but provide us with the means, motive, and opportunity to burn ourselves in a blaze of frantic self-destruction as it whispers in our inner ear that life is naught but pain and death, that existence itself is but a cruel trap on a one-way ride to our own inevitable obliteration. The existential terror induced by this keeps us frozen in a state of suspended animation, too afraid to really live our lives, to allow ourselves to *feel* the full breadth of our emotional experience, with all its attendant pain, *and joy*. As a result, we close ourselves off to our vitality and seal ourselves away, not only from others and the world, but worse still, from our own selves. In an effort to not admit any aspect of life that might inflame our existential suffering, we also shut out any possibility for joyful and intimate connection that could be nourishing and supportive for our taut frozen bodies and terror-stricken psyches.

And just as we won't allow anything or anyone *in* to our frozen fortress of solitude, we also cannot be let *out*. All borders are closed in this cold war of the psyche, under the wary surveillance of the Inner Fascist. From locked within such an ethos of fear, without access to emotional and physical nourishment from intimate, authentic, and vulnerable connection or the supportive freedom to experience and express the full breadth and depth of our emotional vitality, our feeling-function, we either slowly wither or actively participate in our own self-destruction.

As long as the ultimate source of our terror and suffering is our own living system—our finite corpus, our terrorized psyche, our wounded emotions—then we feel that we must, paradoxically, wage war upon ourselves if we are ever to be at peace. Thus proceeds a never-ending cycle that can only serve to increase fear, increase suffering, and seal our demise.

Herein lies the trick and trap of the Inner Fascist: it ends up coercing us into doing to ourselves exactly the harms and abuses from which it is supposed to protect us. It is not our savior or our protector, but the manifestation of the *enemy-within*. *We* end up rejecting and abandoning *ourselves*, *we* coerce and subjugate

138

ourselves, and in the process *we* tragically play a hand in *our own destruction.*

And here we are. From the inside-out, we have wrought our own downfall, as we reckon with this time of dying, at the precipice of this sixth mass extinction. Because regardless of who may yet live, of what species may yet survive this time, our own existence is inexorably tied up with the survival of the collective of every species and ecosystem on this living earth, and thus with every individual life that is at stake. The isolationism of the Inner Fascist is a terrible lie. *We. Are. Not. Separate.* Whosoever dies, we die with them; whosoever survives, we survive *because* of them.

It is ridiculous to think that there can be any "winners" so long as there are "losers." It is ludicrous to ascribe superiority or inferiority of worth since <u>we</u> <u>all</u> <u>need</u> <u>each</u> <u>other</u>.

Win or lose, we do so *together.*

And it is absurd to subscribe to any narrative or paradigm of "us" versus "them," of those of "us" who *belong* and those "others" who do not. Such narrow-minded thinking is a vestige of an antiquated and deeply traumatized perspective of the world, of self and other, which finds its root in the psychological machinations of the Inner Fascist and perpetuates fear, hatred, and violence throughout society, supported by the existing intersectional power structure of imperialist white supremacist capitalist cisheteropatriarchy. If we are to upset the existing power structure, if we want to change the ways that we relate to and with one another, if we hope to live with greater freedom and vitality, inside and out, then we must first and foremost *decolonize* our own minds.

The existing power structure of imperialist white supremacist capitalist cisheteropatriarchy across the globe has more and bigger armies, bombs, guns, and apparatuses of mass surveillance, mass incarceration, and mass death than we could ever—or indeed *should* ever—hope to possess. There is no winning against such a juggernaut. What's more, again, as Audre Lorde taught us, "you cannot dismantle the master's house using the master's tools." As long as we rely on the master's tools of force and coercion, superiority and inferiority, violence and abuse, we will only succeed in rebuilding the master's house again and again. As long as we live from a psychological foundation of fascism, we will only succeed in fomenting fascisms in our relationships and in the world.

We need to decolonize our minds and our hearts; we need to acknowledge, take responsibility for, and deal with the fascist within our own psyches that coerces, violates, and abuses us from within through our own habits of thought and self-talk, and which we then project onto others in the world around us. As within, so without; fascism without is a symptom of fascism within. And thus we cannot attend to the ideological hierarchies and systemic social oppressions in the world unless or until we attend to our own fascistic impulses.

Just as we witness exploitation, subjugation, and violence against vulnerable populations and the earth community expressed through the machinations of the imperialist white supremacist capitalist cisheterpatriarchy, we can also recognize the impulse within ourselves to use, manipulate, ridicule, or even

140

physically harm others in order to get our emotional or physical needs met, or otherwise to gain some sense of security, control, and importance within a profoundly insecure, precarious, depraved, deprived, and dehumanizing social paradigm.

We may not necessarily be aware of such impulses, or we may be reticent to admit their existence even to ourselves, but if we take an honest look at our often subconscious motivations in word, thought, and action, we will find such damaging impulses, even if they contradict our most deeply held values. This self-recognition about how we may be unwittingly causing harm to other people can be deeply painful and elicit a great deal of shame, but it is still not the bottom of the hidden well from which fascism springs—this, too, is but a symptom of a yet deeper fascistic impulse.

At the root of fascism in the outer world, whether in social systems of oppression, exploitation, and violence or in our individual relationships with others, lies the Inner Fascist, that voice that whispers—or shouts—that you will never be good enough, that you are fundamentally unlovable, that you must constantly drive yourself to be better—to "be best"—in order to prove your worth to others and the world, and that if you don't you will die—or worse, live—pathetic and alone.

Ouch. Sound familiar?

But the Inner Fascist is a liar. It tells lies in order to control our thoughts and actions with the twisted logic that following its lead, its commands, will keep us safe from getting hurt or harmed, emotionally or physically. The sad truth, however, is that the Inner Fascist causes us more harm than anyone else could ever do, if for no other reason than it convinces us to betray and belittle our own hearts, our own true natures.

Because the Inner Fascist is not our true nature. It does not originate within the psyche but, like a vicious circle of pain and violence, it seeds itself from the social realm into the personal psyche, and vice versa, thus ensuring its survival in perpetuity. In order to break the cycle of the Inner Fascist we must reject its lies and ground ourselves in truth, the truth that everything in the universe has unconditional value and worth.

In the words of Alfred North Whitehead, "It is the essence of life that it exists for its own sake, as the intrinsic reaping of value."[31] Whitehead further qualifies three fundamental aspects of value or worth, that "of the individual for itself," "of the diverse individuals of the world for each other," and of the "world which is a community."[32] Thus, it is the unconditional nature of nature, of the universe, and thus of us within—or as *manifestations of*— the universe, to value not only self but one another and the whole of our living community. Hence the truth behind the lies of the isolationist Inner Fascist is that the very essence and existence of the manifest universe—and us—is *love*, the longing and desire between all things, the relational interconnection of all existents, which draws us together, as well as forward, in our divine, creative unfolding.

Division and opposition, exploitation and subjugation, superiority and inferiority are all symptoms of an illusion of

---

[31] Whitehead, Alfred North. *Modes of Thought*. Capricorn Books: New York, NY, 1958 [1938], p. 184.
[32] Whitehead, Alfred North. *Religion in the Making*. Fordham University Press: New York, NY, 1996 [1926], p. 59.

separateness, of individualism and alienation, of a me or us versus you or them binary opposition. These are the lies of the fascism which serves to keep us *all* in chains and suffering, whether in body, mind, heart, and/or spirit. Yet this is not simply an effect of human nature, it is not inherent to who we are; rather, it is how we are *not* who we are. It is, in truth, how we become *de*humanized and *in*humane.

CHAPTER NINETEEN

FLOWER-AND-SONG

ENANTIODROMIA: *An ancient Greek term used to describe the tendency of all things to change into their opposite.*

In more modern times, Jung has used this term to explain how psychological balance is restored: when any force within the psyche reaches an extreme, it inevitably produces its opposite. "[T]he more extreme a position is the more easily may we expect an enantiodromia, a conversion of something into its opposite."[33]

This is reflected in the naturalistic *yin-yang* philosophy of the ancient Chinese Taoists. In its early meaning, yin and yang referred to the shaded and sunny sides of a mountain, respectively. We can see the aspect of enantiodromia in this concept when we visualize the mountain in question: what is the shaded, yin, side in the morning turns into its opposite sunny, yang, side in the afternoon; what is the sunny, yang, side in the morning turns into its opposite shaded, yin, side in the afternoon. Yin and yang are opposites in the sense of two complementary halves that make up a larger whole. They are *not* opposites in the sense of antagonistic forces attempting to overcome or destroy one another.

---

[33] *Collected Works*, Vol. 5, par. 581.

On the level of conscious awareness, then, the question is: *How do we contain our own contradiction?*

When the poets and philosophers of ancient Mesoamerica searched for "a place to stand," they ultimately determined that the only authentic cognitive-emotional stance was one they called *Flower-and-Song*.

The questions we face today are no different than those faced by our predecessors: *How do I live authentically? How do I achieve peace of mind without turning my back on those in need? How do I attune myself to the world around me?*

For the ancient Toltecs and the civilizations they inspired, the highest expression of their lifeway was embodied in this mystical philosophy of *Flower-and-Song*.

Flower-and-Song is a *difrasism*, a common form of expression in the Nahuatl language that uses two words to form a metaphor for a third, more expansive concept. *Flower-and-Song* is a metaphor for *Poetry* but its meaning is more comprehensive than that, indicating that its practitioners strive to live a "poetic life" or, more authentically, a "mythic life."

Examining the *difrasism* a little makes this clear:

Flower in this context involves a three-stage engagement with the world. The first stage involves seeing each moment—and whatever that moment holds—as perfect as a blossoming flower. The second stage involves seeing each moment—and whatever that moment holds—as already fading and passing into death. The final stage involves bearing these two visions

146

simultaneously in the heart, engaging the moment and what it holds with the full emotional realization that it is both perfect and dying.

Far from an intellectual exercise, this practice demands the greatest courage, for to face these two soul-shattering emotions at the same time requires us to open ourselves to the profoundest joy and grief all at once. Without flinching from the perfection before us, we are filled with awe at the impossibility of spirit taking form in matter. Without flinching from the inevitable death of everything we know and love, we cannot help but burst apart with grief and empathy.

This is a lifeway, in other words, of spiritual warriors, those who exert constant effort to defeat their self-defeating attitudes and behaviors—the *enemy-within*. It is the lifeway of those who use death to awaken authentic gratitude for being alive and sharing this shape-shifting perfection with others. When we experience it fully, *Flower* evokes a kind of *spiritual nostalgia for the present moment* that ennobles us and all that our lives touch.

Song in this context means that the most authentic act we can perform is to give expression to the dual realization attained in *Flower*. This is the reason that the *difrasism* is generally translated as "poetry." But the deeper implication of this mystical philosophy of life means that *Song* involves treating every moment as an opportunity to express the truth of *Flower*. It involves treating this entire lifetime as a single act of expressing the continuous vision of *Flower*. It means using every thought, word, and deed to embody the lifeway of *Flower-and-Song*.

Treating all things as miracles that pass away too soon, our thoughts, speech, and actions take on a new caliber and timbre. We concentrate on what is present instead of what is absent, and we discover new depths of patience and tolerance. Our lives take on greater meaning and our contributions meet with greater success. We treat everything and everyone more nobly and we are enriched immeasurably.

As a spiritual practice, *Flower-and-Song* enters each moment asking two questions: *What is in front of me? How am I treating it?*

What is in front of me? opens us to the ultimately unknowable nature of the world. By questioning the absolute nature of our perceptions, we come to accept the extraordinary mystery everywhere veiled by ordinary appearances. It is a question that, once taken seriously, forces us to look closer at the world: Is this merely what I have become accustomed to seeing through daily contact—or is it the sea of spirit in all its manifest forms?

How am I treating what is in front of me? demands that we watch our inner actions—our thoughts and intentions, our wishes aimed at things outside ourselves—as well as our outer demeanor and reactions. Am I acting nobly or mean-spiritedly? Am I ennobling my life or trivializing it? Am I rising above pettiness or descending into it? Am I treating others like superiors or inferiors, all in pursuit of my self-interest—or as peers bravely facing their own death as well as they can? Am I spreading ill will, discord and sorrow wherever I go—or compassion, collaboration, and joy?

In our book, *The Toltec I Ching*,[34] Martha Ramirez-Oropeza and I discuss the deeper implications of such a spiritual practice:

> *The spirit warrior breaks through the barrier separating matter and spirit. Such a barrier is erected in our minds by the constant training we receive from those who find advantage in promoting the separation of people from nature, from each other, and from their own true self. If people everywhere perceived matter and spirit to be the same thing, after all, the ignorance, cruelty, and suffering that makes up much of human history would end: if we were all to experience the material form of nature as spirit, we would stop harming it by diminishing it faster than we help it replenish itself; if we were all to experience the material form of people everywhere as spirit, we would stop harming one another by acting as if our own rights and desires were superior to their own; if we were all to experience the material form of our own individual bodies as spirit, we would stop harming ourselves by doubting that every thought, feeling, and action play a pivotal role in eternity. Breaking through such a mental barrier is a matter of constant training as well: if we do not use every thought, feeling, and action to intensify our experience of matter as spirit, we continue to desecrate the temple of nature, the temple of civilization, and the temple of individuality.*

Those following the lifeway of *Flower-and-Song* find that it reveals the wellspring of rejoicing forever bubbling just beneath the surface of appearances. It engages the world as a vast mystery of unimaginable potentials and aims to participate in its

---

[34] Larson Publications, 2009.

ongoing creation in ways that benefit the most. It is not so much something we do on our own as much as it is music we hear and feel and long to play, a dance we cannot wait to join. It arises from our depths to transform the ordinary into the extraordinary.

Holding to such a practice for extended periods of time has certain foreseeable consequences. By forcing us to focus complete attention on *appreciating* the perfection of everything as well as *mourning* its inevitable passing, it trains us to attend fully to the moment, drop off inner talk, participate in life authentically, and honor everything as an equal while knowing it must die.

But it has certain unforeseeable consequences, as well. By blurring the imaginary boundary between self and world, it opens new senses and allows us to perceive the spirit within all matter. By blurring the imaginary line between flawed and flawless, it opens our hearts to the sacredness of all form. By blurring the imaginary boundary between animate and inanimate, it opens our eyes to the formless awareness forever transcending the very form it inhabits. By blurring the imaginary line between time and space, it opens our minds to the unchanging *presence* through which all changing forms move.

The Lifeway of *Flower-and-Song*, then, is a spiritual practice of self-cultivation—it sensitizes us to our tendencies toward self-interest and alienation, replacing self-defeating habits with those of spontaneity, creativity, and good will. It shifts our focus away from personal success toward a heartfelt longing for peace and prospering for all.

And it constantly reminds us that a global Enantiodromia is within our reach if we but dare hold out our hand.

CHAPTER TWENTY

A THEORY OF ENERGY AS GOD

Energy is God. God is energy.

I'm not speaking of the crude kind of fossil fuel energy that makes cars go and the lights turn on—although, remarkably for all the ills it does, that too is a manifestation of God—but rather I am referring to the kind of quantum physical energy that "cannot be created nor destroyed." It cannot be seen, heard, touched, or tasted, but it can be *felt*, experienced, as the living essence that animates the Universe and all its contents.

Though I was raised secular Christian, I never really bought the story about the white, bearded grand-fatherly God who lived in the clouds—to me it was clearly just that: a story. But, nevertheless, I could *feel* that there was more to life than met the physical senses. I fervently believed that there was a "spirit" inside everything, which helped to feed a vibrant imagination and sense of constant companionship—even though as a child I spent much of my time by myself, I never felt alone. The spirits in all the "things" around me, whether animate or inanimate, were as real to me as were their corporeal forms. And even though the finality of death could take those forms away from me and out of the physical world—as with my menagerie of small rodents that I kept as a child, or my dog when I was 10 years old—something in me knew that they weren't really gone, but neither were they in some illusive billowy wonderland called Heaven. They felt closer, like I could reach out anywhere at any time and the spirit of them would still be there in that space and all around me, always.

This sense of Faith has served me countless times since then, and it has evolved over the years from that early childhood conception. My mother—who was raised Catholic but, like me, never subscribed to the traditional notion of God—once encouraged me, back when I was an awkward, anxious and depressed teenager, to "ask the Universe" (her words) for help and guidance. Despite my judgmental teenage cynicism, I took her advice and, looking back, this was the first time that I ever really did anything like "praying," though, at the time, I thought of it more as a kind of meditation.

I was at summer camp at the time, feeling homesick and lonely, not having made any friends yet, and was contemplating coming home early. After a teary, early morning phone conversation with my mother, and at her behest, I sat out on the front porch of the main dining hall and resolved to "ask the Universe."

What I did in that moment, though this may sound paradoxical, was to simultaneously focus and widen my consciousness such that I no longer felt any physical space between me and everything else, even the farthest reaches of the universe. I brought my awareness in to the very center of my own being and, at the same time, out to the infinite vastness of space and held the awareness of both together. From this psychic position, I felt I could communicate directly with a higher force or power by allowing the *feeling* of my dilemma, and the request for help, to flow through my being and, simultaneously, whatever force governs all things.

And amazingly, it worked! After only a short time of this, I heard a door swing open and bang closed loudly, and I opened my eyes to see one of the camp counselors step out onto the porch. He came over and sat down next to me, asked me how I was doing, and we chatted. That one moment opened me up, or perhaps opened the world up to me, because through this experience I recognized that I was not alone, not separate, but held within a vast and communicative intelligence. And to weed away any lingering doubts, by that night I had made at least one tight friend at camp—and many more thereafter—with whom I sat talking late into the night.

I have continued to use this method many times since then for guidance, for comfort, even, at times, for survival. Back then I called this power "the Universe," as had my mother, because it is hence from which we all originate, and what is greater than the vastest reaches of the Universe? If God is anywhere, The[35] must be out there. But I realized that what I was "praying" to wasn't the universe in and of itself—for that is just another manifestation of a power that is greater still and more profound, subtle, and foundational even than the physical universe—but rather the building ground for all living and non-living systems alike. And I realized that the power that I experience flowing through and around me when I bring my attention to the vastness both within and outside of me—aka "the Universe"—is an energetic life-force that animates my body and soul the same

---

[35] "The" is used here as a universal pronoun for God, rather than either of the restrictive and reductive gendered pronouns.

way that it animates the planets and galaxies that expand farther than anyone can ever know. That is what I believe is meant by the term "God" or Allah, Brahman, OM, Orenda (in the indigenous Haudenosaunee language), Gaia, the Tao, Oneness, Source, Essence, the All, or even "the Force" (for any Star Wars fans out there), etc. And it is this energy that I believe answers the ever-present questions: *Where did we come from? What is the "soul" or "spirit" that inhabits the body during life and leaves after death?* Even that ever penetrating conundrum: *Why are we here?*

The answer to the last question, it is my belief, is, simply, to be, to exist. The universe, which is the earliest known manifestation of energy, i.e. God, in material form, exploded forth—as Western materialist science tells us—with a Big Bang, marking the beginning of the evolution of literally everything. This set the process of life in motion—the constellation of dust and fire into stars and planets and galaxies and, eventually, the Earth and, eventually, ecosystems to support animate life and, eventually, amoebas and, eventually, bugs and birds, fish and slugs, lizards and mammals, and, eventually, people too. Through all of this there is a basic process of expansion and contraction, the growth of life and the inevitable decay of death. And thus the movement and transfer of energy continues to flow throughout all things.

This is the basic principle of Life: movement, transition, change, the constant flow of energy in, through, and around everything, through the processes of growth and decay, for eons. And when I ask myself why—why any of this? The answer inevitably comes—*because.* Simply that: because. Because it is what it is. Because there is something very sacred about this process, about

Life, and death, and about the Energy that underlies and animates it all, this seemingly endless dance of Beingness.

And that's the only reason that I ever need.

CHAPTER TWENTY-ONE

A NEW SOCIAL CONTRACT

Spiritually-minded people seek to establish social and political systems that institutionalize the ideals of *humaneness and justice*. People who lack this perspective seek to establish social and political systems that protect the upper class and suppress the lower class.

My personal experience living among Indigenous people for two years taught me that the former ideal can be achieved. It works because social rituals demonstrating and reinforcing mutual respect dissolve classism, institutionalizing *self-control* among all members of the community. It creates a social world of *enlightened anarchy*, in which individuals have freedom of behavior so long as it does not impinge upon another's. This leads, in my experience, to the highest degree of eccentricity and idiosyncratic attitudes and behaviors—which is to say, creativity and adaptability—constrained only by the social norm of mutual respect.

Obviously, such a system does not prevent differences from arising. The mechanism that holds people together even in conflict is twofold:

- their faith in an impartial mediator able to arbitrate the needs and interests of members in such a way as to consistently reinforce the coherence of the community;

159

- their commitment to abiding by the mediator's judgment.

When I returned to life in modern society, one of the first things I did was to take formal training as a mediator. My instructor had been practicing the craft for decades and carried not just knowledge of the craft, but wisdom of the art. His emphasis on impartiality struck me as a mental-emotional training laying a foundation for ethical action in the work of conflict resolution.

It got me to thinking:

When the present out-of-balance civilization inevitably collapses, what will we replace it with?

Should a civilization of *enlightened anarchy* arise, how could it fulfill the ideal of *humaneness and justice* and sustain it over a long period of time?

I can envision such a culture: based on twin principles of *community-binding*—mutual respect and self-control—a global civilization of enlightened anarchy could function if all its laws, governments, and armies were replaced by a ubiquitous corps of *ordained mediators*.

You can see by the word *ordained* that something resembling a monk-like training would prepare individuals for the rigors of their social and political role. Part psychologist, part diplomat: such mediators would need to possess a profound understanding of human nature, as well as an unshakeable impartiality devoted first and foremost to humaneness and justice. The training would need to cultivate certain positive personality traits,

160

beginning with humility as exemplified in the axiom: *It is the robe, not the person.*

Beyond the mediators' training, the culture itself would need to be grounded in a new *social contract*—one of abiding by the decisions of the mediators. Toward that end, much of the knowledge-base of the mediators' training would infuse the general education system, instilling in people from a young age the attitudes and behaviors of conflict resolution. This would add a *willingness to compromise* to the fundamental social responsibilities: *mutual respect* and *self-control.*

All this implies a social contract of community-binding. Like the tributaries of a great river, individuals must lead themselves to common goals in concert with others. And since people have different concerns, goals need to be identified by their different levels of conflict resolution—which would define the levels of intervention for which mediators were trained:

> individual crises
> personal relationships
> local community
> organizations
> national
> international

Since different co-leaders would inevitably envision different courses of interaction toward the same goal, they would have to adopt different kinds of mediation in order to maintain their cooperative strategies. And that would be even more important when multiple efforts toward goals that appear to be at odds with one another emerge. We would have to model training on

161

cultivating the attitude and behavior of water and soil and sunlight, nurturing every seed without preference, allowing the most beneficial and best adapted to ultimately prevail.

It is never too early to begin training a worldwide corps of mediators since that could well play the pivotal role in a new social contract of *cooperative anarchy*. We would all benefit from exposure to an emerging curriculum articulating a whole new vision of humaneness, justice, mutual respect, self-control, and compromise.

Pura Vida.

CHAPTER TWENTY-TWO

SPIRITUAL ANARCHY OR THE INNER FASCIST

PART III

Fascism is the result of a distortion of our human faculty of ego-consciousness.

The function of what psychologists have come to call the ego—which is, as far as we know in the history of mammals, a distinctly human phenomenon—is to differentiate and discern, and thus to be able to reflect upon the world—in a word: to *think*. With this capacity, however, comes an experience of separation between subject and object, "in here" and "out there," and thus between self and "other," or self and the world. And here, again, we encounter the pitfall of the *thinking-function*, that of dissociation and the resultant alienation from others and the world with whom we are relationally bound and inextricably interdependent.

But when we think about others or the world "out there" as distinct from ourselves "in here" they become alien to us, and thus they are perceived as a potential foe or threat to our security. Such a sense of insecurity is a manifestation of a weak or fragile ego-consciousness, which triggers a perceived need to assert dominance through coercion, ridicule, exploitation, and/or physical violence. Hence, the enacting of bigotry and othering based on race, religion, nationality, gender, sexuality, and other superficial differences; hence, competition between supposedly disparate groups; hence, the concept of "winners" and "losers"; hence, a dialectic of superiority and inferiority which lends itself to subjugation and exploitation of the "losers" by the "winners"; hence, the existence and historical precedents of rape, slavery, poverty, social ostracism, genocide, and all forms of social oppression and bullying.

But it does not have to be this way. Such atrocities are not endemic to human nature. The egoic capacity to discern does not have to lead to competition, bigotry, and exploitation. The capacity to discern is necessary in order to have a sense of self and thus of self-awareness and self-reflection, but that awareness of self, of one's individuality, does not have to be at odds with "others." Rather, that egoic capacity allows us to know ourselves as a *unique and crucial part* of a *relational whole*.

Without egoic consciousness there is simply the immanently experiencing whole—one mind, one perspective, one body. With egoic consciousness that whole is able to become pluralistically self-reflective through the myriad diverse individual expressions of itself. The individual expresses wholeness while the whole reflects unique individuality through its parts; there is no part without the whole, no whole without the parts. From the perspective of egoic consciousness the whole is able to look back at itself through the experiences of the parts and *know* itself. But neither the whole nor the individual can know itself so long as it remains deluded by an illusion of separateness, of an individuality dissociated from the whole, from the collective, from "other."

Self and other, self and world, individual and collective, part and whole are inextricably relationally bound. This is the eternal paradox of fate and free will: as individual (parts) we have the freedom to creatively determine our unfolding destiny, to *choose* our thoughts and actions. But those thoughts and actions are also always bound to and limited by the needs and concessions, or opportunities, of the social collective (whole) in which we exist. An individual can privately choose to enact infinite possibilities of thought, word, and action—this is the genius of art and the ideal of free expression—but those thoughts, words, and actions will always take place within a public context of the time, locality, culture, and mores of the society in which the individual lives.

Thus, every thought, word, and action of every individual adds something of creative genius to the public context, to the status quo, but every thought, word, and action also depends upon the public for its reception (or rejection), and thus for its impact and endurance. No deed stands alone. Thus, with great freedom of the individual must come great responsibility to the collective whole. This is how we experience our belonging, which necessitates both a community to offer receptive welcome and support, and an individual to be welcomed, to be received.

It is from such a relational perspective—not from a dissociated, isolated individualism, but from a *fundamentally connected, deeply embedded mutual reciprocation*—that the human egoic consciousness can thrive from a sense of security based in acceptance and valuation, rather than wither from a devastating

165

sense of insecurity and defensiveness in a climate of division, alienation, and hierarchy. As opposed to the fragile ego-structure which leads to insecurity and divisiveness, such a relational context instead breeds a resilient ego-structure founded in a sense of unconditional security in and valuation of oneself in the collective that is not dependent either on other's "right" conduct or their approval. Such a position of security negates any sense of need to coerce, control, or dominate others in order to stay safe from their actions, or to coerce, control, or betray *ourselves* in order to gain others' conditional admiration and acceptance.

So long as we subscribe to the narrative of superiority and inferiority, then any perceived rejection or contradiction of our "rightness" is experienced as a confirmation of our inadequacies, or our worthlessness. If we believe that we can only be good, be valued—be "Something that matters!"[36]—so long as we can prove our worth to others, to the collective, to the status quo, to the Inner Fascist, then *we are our own colonizers*. Then we betray our own true natures, our hearts and spirits, the creative expression of our unique and important manifestation of the unfolding Universal Life Force.

And as long and as far as we reject, violate, and betray our own dignity and integrity of Being, then we will inevitably visit that same intolerance, rejection, and *violence* upon other people and into the world. Because it is a *violence* that we do to ourselves when we take the side of the Inner Fascist over our own divinely immanent sacred integrity. It is a violation and a betrayal of self,

---

[36] Whitehead, Alfred North. *Modes of Thought*. Capricorn Books: New York, NY, 1958 [1938], p. 159.

just as acts of violence and systems of oppression and exploitation are a violation and a betrayal of others' sacred integrity.

We have the power and the capacity within us, as part of our sacred integrity, our divinely immanent creative unfolding, to *choose* to resist the seductive whispers of the Inner Fascist, to repudiate the narrative of superiority and inferiority, to resolve to love and accept ourselves unconditionally, and to love and accept others *as ourselves*.

In place of the old coercive and exploitative paradigm of both inner and outer fascisms, we can choose instead to cultivate a *Spiritual Anarchy*.

Why "anarchy"? Because anarchy means something more than simply "no rulers." Nor is it just a synonym for chaos. In its sincerest form, anarchy is order without oppression, community without coercion, freedom without isolation or alienation, equality without homogeneity, and sustainability without exploitation.

Anarchy supports *freedom* of expression and feeling, of the individual to be fully and authentically true to one's nature and spirit, at the same time that it upholds the freedom of expression of others to be true to their own natures, spirits, and cultures;

Anarchy promotes *solidarity* between all living beings as interdependent co-constituents within an inclusive community of local and global, social and ecological systems;

Anarchy supports the *co-creative* generation of relevant, adequate, and consensual social systems as necessary to the *reciprocal and equitable* care for the whole community.

Ultimately, anarchy recognizes that *with great freedom comes great responsibility*, and that we must utilize our individual freedoms for the greatest *benefit* according to the greatest *needs* of the whole community. It may seem paradoxical that without communal solidarity, without supporting the collective, personal freedoms cannot flourish, or they become distorted and destructive. Anarchy embraces this paradox.

But this requires that we do the deeply personal work of reckoning with the Inner Fascist, of developing a strong egoic consciousness that cultivates a profound and resilient sense of integrity—of *integration*—both in oneself and with the whole, in place of a fragile egoic consciousness that seeks for the promise of superiority over others in order to feel secure. We must face and acknowledge the ways in which we not only allow ourselves to be divided from one another in society, but the ways that we allow ourselves to be divided and dismembered within and from our own selves; the ways in which we not only perpetrate abuse, harm, ridicule, and violence upon others, but the ways that we perpetrate self-abusive thoughts and behaviors, self-harm, self-ridicule, and the violence of punitive shame and self-loathing against ourselves. This is the devastation wrought by the Inner Fascist that ripples out into society from within its stronghold in our own minds, lurking in the shadows of our own subconscious.

In the face of the Inner Fascist, the courageous and radical practice of *integration* which recognizes a real relational ethic of universal mutual reciprocity must be fundamentally founded in unconditional *love and acceptance* of self; *respect* for others' individuality and unique expressions and experiences, including cultural, racial, gender, and other differences; a *willingness to engage and connect* across said differences; and a commitment to *build relationships of commonality* across difference rather than foment divisions of tribalistic protectionism along exclusionary lines.

Neither the Inner Fascist nor social fascisms can survive in a psychosocial landscape of Spiritual Anarchy, in which we know that we are never truly alone and cannot be divided or abandoned because we are inherently connected and held within a loving and respectful web of relations.

The intellectual acknowledgement, somatic felt experience, and deep spiritual knowing of our *unconditional Belonging* to this web of relations negates any impetus for comparison and valuation, for perpetuating narratives and paradigms of superiority and inferiority, for forcing ourselves to be what we are not, to live up to some inauthentic and false ideal of impossible rectitude and righteous authority. We can, rather, relax into and en*joy* the simple fact of our existence, our unique and precious finite experience, to *feel* ourselves and the world around us through the sacred sublime experience of *living* as an integral expression of an immanent whole.

Concordantly, the recognition of a so-called "other" as an extension of oneself negates any impetus to ostracize, demean, or dehumanize. We can instead recognize that any harm done to others is inevitably done to ourselves, and vice versa, and that insofar as we can love and accept ourselves, we can love and accept others as well.

This is not some Pollyannaish plea or platitude—the serious *work* of defying the Inner Fascist and choosing instead to align with self-love and acceptance is radical, courageous, and paradigm shifting. It has the power to alter the very fabric of our reality, both internally and externally, personally and socially. It has the power to *change the world.*

Standing in and moving from this new anti-fascist psychosocial landscape of Spiritual Anarchy, we find that not only are *we* held in and *belong* to an inextricable web of relations, but so too are those around us, so too are *all others*—that in fact *we need and belong to each other.* This is what is meant by mutual reciprocity. This is what solidarity looks like. This is what solidarity *feels* like.

It is when our global social landscape matches this inner landscape; when—through our radical, courageous, and sustained work of loving self as other and other as self, and trusting in the universal matrix of unconditional Belonging— that we find ourselves living outwardly a social ethic of anarchy seeded by Spiritual Anarchy.

When *all* beings are valued and respected for their unique expressions, then, and only then, can we truly say that "all lives matter." But as long as we continue to perpetuate a fascistic social landscape of superiority and inferiority, of division and fear, predicated on the racist and chauvinistic violence of the existing imperialist white supremacist capitalist cisheterpatriarchal power structure, then any assertion that "all

170

lives matter" is merely a petty defense of that order, and thus of fascism itself. This is why—in this day and age when the existing power structure does not, in thought, word, or deed, value all lives equitably—to say that "all lives matter" in response to the assertion—the plea—that "Black Lives Matter" is, in fact, a defense of racism and white supremacy; it is, in a word, racist because it is a reification and a perpetuation of anti-Blackness and white supremacy within the psychosocial landscape.

These now times—these times of dying—require a radical new way of *living*. But this new way of living is still in the process of being discovered. From within the old narratives and paradigms we are simply groping in the dark, waiting for our eyes to adjust to a new way of seeing and thus relating to our world, ourselves, and one another.

Living in a time of dying requires a radical evolution. Billions of years ago, prokaryotic bacteria evaded extinction when, in the final crucial moments of the first mass extinction, they learned to metabolize the tremendous amounts of oxygen—O_2—that had been created from their own photosynthetic activity, and which was now threatening to extinguish these first vestiges of life on earth.[37] How ironic then, that like our oldest ancestors, those early bacteria, we have created an atmospheric force—now CO_2—that again threatens to destabilize and extinct much of the now myriad and complex living organisms and ecosystems on this planet. Where those earliest life forms

---

[37] Swimme, Brian & Berry, Thomas. *The Universe Story: From the Primordial Flaring Forth to the Ecozoic Era: A Celebration of the Unfolding of the Cosmos.* Harper Collins: San Francisco, 1992.

survived extinction by inventing the mechanism of breathing, now, from smog-choked cities to smoke-choked countrysides to the Covid-19 pandemic to the now infamous last words of Eric Garner and George Floyd, people all over the world are pleading: "I can't breathe."

And while I can't speak to the political machinations or intrigues of bacteria, *we* humans have devised diabolical systems of division and animosity between ourselves which now not only impairs our ability to connect and come together under such dire circumstances, but it has made our experience of *living* itself a hell on earth. Regardless of whether one finds oneself in the upper echelons of a superiority-inferiority-based social order, or under the boot—or knee—of those who are, we all suffer profound insecurity, fear, defensiveness, and isolationism under a fundamentally inhumane system. We are all forced to struggle for power, for supremacy, for the right to survive, much less thrive, under the death-cult that is imperialist white supremacist capitalist cisheteropatriarchy—that is white supremacist hatred; that is cisheterpatriarchal violence and control; that is imperialist racial capitalism; that is fascism in all its forms. Not only is it morally corrupt, not only is it socially unjust, not only is it psychologically traumatizing, not only is it physically violent, not only is it spiritually demoralizing, but such a world-order is wholly and completely *unnecessary*.

It does not have to be this way. The current paradigm does not serve anyone, except as an ultimately fragile, transitory, and illusory façade or mirage of power, importance, and control. In truth, it only *harms* all of us to uphold such a delusional and divisive binary narrative and fascistic paradigm. But to defeat fascism in the world we must *heal* the fascistic impulses within

172

our own psyches, through a radical commitment to *love*, *compassion*, and *respect*.

Imagine what it could be like to not live in shame, self-loathing, and a persistent fear of social rejection and/or oppression; to not have to fight or sell ourselves in order to survive; to not have to compete against others simply for the right to exist. Imagine, rather than feeling alienated and afraid of "others," what it could be like to instead feel a sense of deep Belonging to a Beloved Community.[38]

We must *envision* this new narrative and with it a new world in which all people, including queer, trans, and Black, Indigenous, and other peoples of color, of all ages, sizes, and abilities, have access to the resources they need to live safe and fulfilling lives; in which the supremacy and powers of whiteness and cismaleness are abolished and queer, femme, and all bodies of color are accepted and protected; in which we are all considered full citizens of a global community and arbitrary borders no longer separate us and demarcate who may receive necessary resources, care, and support; in which we cooperate in global solidarity rather than attempt to dominate and/or exploit our neighbors; in which everyone's physical, emotional, mental, and spiritual integrity is honored; in which nonhuman animals, organisms, and ecosystems are treated as equally valuable and inextricably essential to human life; in which the exploitative economic system of capitalism is replaced with one based instead on an ethic of care and universal mutual reciprocity; in which differences between people are respected and valued; in which individual free expression is supported as an act of vital

---

[38] Credit for this term and concept is due to the philosopher Josiah Royce.

creative fulfillment; in which *love* is what moves us, what draws us, compels us, ever together and ever forward in the sacred mandate of our unfolding potential.

We cannot create what we cannot first imagine. We must break our own hearts, minds, and spirits out of the old narrative of superiority and inferiority, hatred and fear, and begin the courageous work of dreaming the as yet unknown into being.

CHAPTER TWENTY-THREE

REAL VICTORY

The wise assimilate the opposition.

Confrontation and conflict merely play into the hands of the invisible rulers: Anonymous Power rules by fabricating ideological extremes and setting them against one another in an ongoing culture war that distracts the populace from ever uniting against their common oppressor.

The wise know the opposition better than they know themselves. The wise understand the common ground they share with the opposition and speak to them in the language of symbols that reach their hearts. The wise do not seek to defeat the opposition—they seek to make of them great-souled allies; they see them as noble warriors standing for what they hold most valuable and most worth preserving.

The wise take the long view, knowing that humaneness and justice will inevitably evolve and progressively resolve civilization's most difficult problems. The wise do not speak aloud about radical immediate change, as this inflames the reactionary elements of the opposition and creates a backlash that actually impedes change and prolongs the time it takes to implement it.

The wise act nonetheless in a timely fashion, recognizing the seeds of opposition growing and so move to assimilate them before they grow and require an exponentially greater effort.

The wise know that great pyramids are built one stone at a time. And that they are built by a sustained collective, collaborative, effort. The wise seek to build a civilization that is a worthy monument to human nature—one that endures because it embodies a harmonious balance both among all people as well as between civilization and the natural environment.

The wise know that vested interests hold hidden power and influence, so that change moves with less friction if their interests can be incorporated into the emerging social-political-economic order.

The wise understand that good endings beget good beginnings: transitions are all-important. The timing of each step is as much a matter of sage improvisation as of intelligent planning. Efficiency is of less importance than people: gradual erosion often accomplishes what a sudden blow does not.

The wise understand that good beginnings beget good endings: great wrongs have been perpetuated down through the ages—nothing can undo those wrongs, but their causes can be ended in the present. This requires a deep sensitivity to and clear insight of the detrimental effects such wrongs have wrought: people on all sides must strive to communicate from the heart, working together to right wrongs without committing more wrongs.

The wise neither take offense nor give offense. They do not make enemies, nor do they allow others to name them enemy.

They build alliances that serve the best interests of all and are based on sincere good will and mutual respect. They listen, they do not preach. They learn, they do not correct. They strive to rid themselves of righteous indignation and inculcate within themselves enduring tolerance.

The wise see solidarity where others see opposition. They do not allow others to become the "other" of their own unconscious. They know that not all noble-hearted people agree on every point. They welcome compromise as a way to proceed while hoping to persuade others to their point of view, even as they use that time to honestly stay open to being persuaded to another's point of view.

The wise know the power of terrorism and dissent. They strive to build a living, evolving whole of such beauty and worth that its people can withstand and absorb shocks without being triggered into kneejerk reactions they later regret. If something is aimed at forcing a backlash, then every effort ought to be made to resist such predictability. Solidarity among people based on a heartfelt love of their lifeway builds an elevated sense of community immune to being torn apart from either the inside or the outside.

The wise know the power of children and imagination. The ability to assimilate opposition arises from the ability of individuals to integrate their own contradictory nature, especially the ability to recognize their own psychological-emotional shadow as a living part of themselves. They know that the way of educating children has to be based on opening their minds to accepting not all known possibilities, but the unknown ones as well—to prepare people from the very beginning to the positive creative potential unleashed by uniting opposites. The wise do not try to domesticate human nature by limiting its vision of the world and its own creative potential— rather, they nurture the wild and untamed spirit of imagination forever pressing at the frontier of curiosity, wonder, and awe.

The wise do not strive to defeat their own highest hopes, deepest desires, gravest fears, most haunting griefs: they incorporate all the unattainable perfections and unavoidable imperfections into a living, evolving civilization embodying a meaningful lifeway for all.

The wise do not identify with either of the extremes—they identify with the center. The wise occupy the center, continually integrating the extremes into a cohesive and meaningful whole instead of continually setting them against one another in mutually destructive conflict.

The wise assimilate the real opposition.

CHAPTER TWENTY-FOUR

WHAT IT IS

One summer day, after a long hot afternoon working in the garden, I took a respite laying on my back in the grass and gazed up at the sky through the gently tilting leaves of an aspen grove. Bees and other insects buzzed lazily around the branches, birds chirped and alighted from here to there, the air was thick and humid with the breath of growing things, and the rays of the sun twinkled off the silvery leaves. I felt the soft though solid earth beneath me, teeming and alive, and the tickle of grasses against my skin, as well as the odd fly or ant venturing to scale my mountainous body.

As I lay there in rapt wonderment at the fecund beauty and sensuous pleasure of nature in its season of abundant vitality, I recalled a recent conversation with my dear friend and teacher, William Douglas Horden, in which he had mused how everything we think we perceive is really just quanta popping in and out of existence. I know this to be true, scientifically, and yet my direct perceptions—of the trees, the bugs, the grass and solid ground, the warm rays of the sun—are so convincing!

So I attempted, in that moment, to soften those perceptions—not to imagine, per se, but to simply allow for the possibility that what I was seeing and feeling—myself included—was in fact rather an immense cloud of subatomic quanta whirling, humming, and snapping, and from this nebulous cloud of potentia arise shapes and forms, the perceptive experience of trees and bugs, light and air, ground and grass, and yes, even me.

The feeling that arose was both tremendously exhilarating and ecstatically peaceful. Like breathing underwater. Like floating in a vast ocean. Like being held. I was simultaneously a part within this cosmic soup and one *with* it—my own body as vastly effervescent as the cosmos itself.

Laying on my back in the grass expanding my awareness in an attempt to try to conceive of the fabric of reality—and myself within it—as quanta popping and whirling in and out of existence, unfurling in a cosmic dance of being and becoming, I felt myself (literally, *my self*) diffuse as if I had become aerosolized. The bounds of my body no longer existed, the whole universe flowed through me as easily as water. My awareness of my self dropped to the background, like the vague memory of a dream. I was not me, this distinct, finite creature, not exactly, but the instantiation of the whole cosmos.

I reveled in this epiphany for several moments before my mind got the better of me and coaxed me back to my garden chores. Reluctantly, though feeling quite revived by my momentary reverie, I hauled myself to my feet and attempted to wield my body through space.

The world reeled around and underneath me! I felt myself as a giant as I took a few halting steps, unsure that the ground would be there to meet my weight.

I laughed out loud, first at the absurdity of trying to maneuver as a universe in such a tight little form, and then at the sheer joy of experiencing myself *as* the universe. I had tricked my brain out of its illusion of my own small, separate, finitude, and for that moment I had experienced a profound freedom and deep sense of security: the truth of what is.

CHAPTER TWENTY-FIVE

THE TAO OF GREEN

When the world is governed according to Tao,
Horses are used to work the land.
When the world is not governed according to Tao,
Warhorses and weapons are sent to the frontier.
There is no greater calamity than lavish desires.
There is no greater guilt than discontentment.
There is no greater disaster than greed.
Those who are contented with contentment
Always have enough.

~ Tao Te Ching, Chapter 46

The inevitable fully green society is not simply waiting for the reformation of social institutions that have vested interest in maintaining the status quo.

If only it were that easy.

No, what the inevitable fully green society is waiting for is the transformation of human nature.

We are not going to be able to rein in the powerful institutions that stand in the way until we rein in the worst traits of humanity—those that allow us to desecrate nature and exploit our fellow human beings without conscience or thought of the long-range consequences. I find that Taoism is particularly timely in addressing the dilemmas we face through its profound love of both humanity and nature.

Taoism is the indigenous lifeway of ancient China, a philosophy based on bringing people into accord with the Tao, or Way, that guides and sustains all form from within. Like many other schools of thought that seek to ground individuals in the living reality of nature and psyche, Taoism begins with the traditional recognition that the Way is beyond the rational mind's grasp of words and ideas.

> *The Tao that can be spoken is not the Tao itself.*
> *The name that can be given is not the name itself.*
> *The unnameable is the source of the universe.*
> . . .
> *Its wonder and manifestations are one and the same.*
> *Since their emergence, they have been called by different names.*
> *Their identity is called the mystery.*
> *From mystery to further mystery:*
> *The entry of all wonders!*

> ~ *Tao Te Ching*, Chapter 1

This famous passage introduces several key points that make it particularly well-adapted to green philosophy. First, it recognizes that there exists a mysterious immaterial force at work in the on-going creation of matter and life. Second, it recognizes that its *spiritual wonder* and *material manifestations* are one and the same. And third, it recognizes that focusing on

184

the self-sameness of spirit and matter is the Way to a personal, first-hand experience of the unnameable source of the universe.

In short, we are brought into accord with the immaterial source of creation when we experience all matter as spirit. Seeing that everything physical *is* the sacred necessarily alters our perception of self and other, drawing us into the oceanic experience of the non-duality of the One. If all matter, in other words, is seen as sacred, then it becomes morally impossible to treat it otherwise: neither other people nor nature can be intentionally harmed.

Without this first-hand experience of the self-sameness of nature and psyche, it is easy for us to slip into either the kind of base materialism that rejects the validity of anything beyond the senses or the kind of spiritual nihilism that rejects the validity of the world of the senses. The Tao, as the ever-present union of opposites, balances and harmonizes extremes, bringing everything back to center over the long run, so that there is nothing that is not eventually the Way. We are brought into accord with the Tao, then, when we sensitize ourselves to its unitary nature by cultivating a profound and equal respect for matter and spirit.

As might be expected, such a balanced philosophy of life has developed a well-articulated code of ethics:

> *When the world is governed according to Tao,*
> *Horses are used to work the land.*
> *When the world is not governed according to Tao,*
> *Warhorses and weapons are sent to the frontier.*
> *There is no greater calamity than lavish desires.*

185

There is no greater guilt than discontentment.
There is no greater disaster than greed.
Those who are contented with contentment
Always have enough.

It is in this practical application of the Tao that we see the intimate connection between government, nature, and individual responsibility.

When government is guided by a sense of the sacredness of everything, then our interaction with nature is one of harmony and gratitude for our sustenance. When government lacks a sense of the sacred, however, the same resources are turned toward aggression and dominance. Such impropriety on the part of government can only be countermanded by society supporting the very best in its individuals. Making *contentment* the highest value rather than wealth, status, or fame is the necessary re-valuing of values that offers us the surest road to a self-sustaining lifeway that celebrates a time of peace and prospering for all.

It is lavish desires, discontent, and greed, after all, that fuel the fire of war. Only when we personally experience these attributes as the cause of the greatest calamity, deepest guilt, and darkest disaster do we voluntarily place the well-being of the Whole ahead of our private self-interest. The vision of the One is based on the Taoist precept that *everything we know about spirit we have learned by analog from nature*.

The One is, like the rainforest, a riot of plurality, a celebration of diversity. It is a unity of neither uniformity nor conformity. It encourages and rewards the exploration of potential individual

186

forms. The One is the ever-present force of coherence, the indwelling essence holding things together: it is not hierarchical, it is relational. When we name it, we call it the universal path, the common Way, upon which all creation moves. When we experience its immaterial presence, we are attuned to the Underlying Harmony of civilization and nature. The products of our own handiwork, both technological and artistic, then *fit* with our environment's creations and reveal to us our own sacred nature.

Now, of course, some people will argue that discontent is the force that drives people to discover better things and is the very heart of progress. The counter-argument to this is that simply creating new things is not in and of itself progress—without the wisdom to know what *not* to do, we do not progress but engage in self-destructive behaviors that not only harm our own lives but those of the generations to come. Treating matter as dead inorganic material and plants and animals solely as resources for our own well-being is a terrible act of violence against creatures who perfected their adaptation to the world long before we appeared on the scene.

The inevitable fully green global society is growing not simply out of the need to design a self-sustaining lifeway. It is part of the emerging world culture whose self-governance is rooted in the shared personal experience of the sacredness of everything. As originally conceived and expressed, the Tao is the creative force Itself working from inside every creation—to experience the Tao, we need only find it within ourselves; to express It, we need only give it free rein to act naturally. By acting like nature, setting our intent on *The Benefit Of All* like water and soil and sunlight, we move beyond self-destructive self-interest and embody enlightened self-interest. Then, and only then, Taoism proposes, will we be *content with contentment* and always have enough.

Chapter Twenty-Six

Encounter with a Dreamer

Part I

I am on the top floor of a five-story building with my brother. We are the only two there. The floor plan is wide open, with three of the exterior walls made of floor to ceiling glass. It is just past dusk and the brightest stars are beginning to twinkle. I go to one of the windows and look up. I call my brother over to point out where all of the five closest planets are visible in the sky.

"Look, see? There is Mercury," I say, pointing.

But just next to Mercury is another light, not a planet or a star but a satellite. I can tell because it is moving fast. But it is also getting brighter, larger. I realize with shock that it is not moving East to West, but growing steadily nearer, on a crash course for Earth.

It enters the atmosphere and streaks across the sky. My brother and I run to the Easterly window to watch in horror for where it will land. I am terrified that it may hit a populated area and pray for it to land somewhere remote. It streaks past our window, too far to the left to see—its landing is obscured by the one opaque wall to the North. I press myself up against the glass to try to get a glimpse of its final impact, but I cannot see.

Just as I am sure it lands, I see a light grow from the direction of its crash, but this is something else. It grows

189

as a mushroom cloud, but bigger still. I know that it is from the Earth itself, an explosion of magma to rent the bedrock. This is it. The Earth's demise, or final release, with all of us with it.

Time seems to slow down. I know what is coming—the wave of heat and radiation that will obliterate everything in its path. I wonder what it will feel like—will I feel it? Or will it be so quick that I won't even notice? I realize with a deep wave of grief and love that it is not only I who will die, but everyone and everything that I have ever known and held dear; that there will be no after, no mourning, no "life goes on." All of it, the entire Earth, will be, simply, gone.

And then it comes, like a burst of air. There is no pain. The world around me fades to white.

I find myself wondering, in these final milliseconds stretching in time, when my consciousness will cease, and what will it be like to die?

And then there is, simply, nothing, but peace.

I relayed this dream to my new friend. He's an avid and practiced lucid dreamer and so I inquire as to his interpretation. At the time we are speeding down the highway in Northern California toward San Francisco, having only met the day before at a semi-annual retreat for our graduate program in Philosophy, Cosmology, and Consciousness (PCC) at the California Institute of Integral Studies (CIIS). We are students in the online cohort of the program, living at a distance from San Francisco, where the school is based. He has been kind enough to give me and another classmate a ride back to the city and we three use the opportunity of the car ride to share our stories and our passions, what brought us to this program, and what particular interests beckon our curiosities and aspirations.

Within our sacred little community of philosophers, mystics, and visionaries, one often finds oneself engaged in esoteric conversation—not only on the abstract ontologies and epistemologies of the Western philosophical canon, but on topics such as Eastern mysticism and indigenous wisdom teachings, quantum physics, hallucinogenics and holotropic states, even magic and astrology. Alternative and altered ways of knowing are not taboo here, but are respected and affirmed as not only valid, but important, crucial even, to the evolutionary unfolding of human consciousness, as well as social justice and ecological sustainability. We are asked and encouraged to call forth and take seriously what lies in our dreams and in our hearts, as it is from such innate intelligence that we will envision and dream a new world into being—one that does not denigrate and destroy living beings and systems for the frivolous and iniquitous pursuit of profit and power; one that instead affirms and respects the vital integrity—and integral vitality—of the many and the One whole, of the physical world with its divine immanence, and of the existential sanctity of all.

The day prior a group of us had taken a short hike into the arid hills of Sonoma County. I was new to the program and didn't yet know many people, and so I followed along quietly listening to the casual but animated discussions among my new colleagues. Upon reaching a small shady landing we took a brief respite to decide whether to continue on ahead or turn back in time for the next scheduled lecture.

Just then a tall lanky bearded fellow to my left turned to me, extended a hand, and said, "I don't think we've met yet. I'm Matt."

"Matt Flowers?" I replied.

"Yeah!" he responded, his bushy Muir-esque beard breaking with a wide warm smile.

"You have a memorable name," I told him. "I'm Meghan Tauck."

I would be lying if I said that from that moment on I wasn't eminently aware of his presence. I hardly remember the topic of conversation on our walk back through the hot and dusty California wood, but if I close my eyes I can feel myself there, and him walking just behind me and to my right in our small cluster of new acquaintances, as if there was but the thinnest veil separating that day from this.

~

Matt had spent the last fifteen years studying the art—for it is an art—of lucid dreaming. He was also somewhat of an adventurer, having traveled and lived for a time in South America, where he had taught English, and now living in Los Angeles where he taught Spanish and enjoyed the companionship of his long-time childhood friends from Oklahoma, where he had been raised. Now, as we speed down the 101, he confesses that he realized he had spent too many years being frivolous with his life—partying and doing drugs just for the fun of it, rather than as sacred conduits to a higher plain of awareness—and that he is

192

endeavoring, through his graduate studies, to seriously apply himself to his lucid dreaming practice and to the pursuit and evolution of consciousness.

I, too, shared my own story: I had come to the program by way of my astrological studies, which I had come to through a deep personal crisis fifteen years prior, when I had become very ill with an auto-immune condition that had brought my erstwhile life to a staggering halt. Through the process of unwinding and healing my physical ailments, astrology had offered me a stalwart sense of faith that had buoyed me through this dark period by giving me a sense of meaning and, indeed, of purpose in what otherwise seemed a cruel and miserable waste of my life.

Prior to my illness I had been attending college in New York City, studying critical race theory and education, and had plans of working as an organizer and activist for social justice. In the wake of my experiences on September 11, 2001, however, I had become increasingly anxious and agitated, suffering chronic nightmares and panic attacks due to post-traumatic stress, and was forced to withdraw from school and move back home with my family. It was then that my health too began to fail, making it impossible for me to remain academically or socially active and thus thwarting whatever ideas I had for my future. I was thrust into uncharted territory with no map or direction.

In an attempt to better understand my psycho-somatic condition—and, really, due to a deep instinctual calling—I began studying Jungian and transpersonal psychology and other mystical traditions, as well as pursued astrological guidance. In the decade-and-a-half since, I had dedicated myself to the study of psychological and esoteric traditions that elucidated not only the machinations of the human unconscious, but the foundations, the ground, the wellspring of *consciousness* itself, including the energy body that is its vessel in this material plain of existence. All of this had prepared me, in my own unique way, for advanced study in Philosophy, Cosmology, and Consciousness (although I joked that I had come to the program for the Cosmology and Consciousness, but quickly found out that I first had to wade through the dense canon of Philosophy to get to them...).

I had chosen this program because I saw that it weaved together so many of the various threads of inquiry that I had pursued over the years—from Jungian psychology, to history and anthropology, to quantum physics, to consciousness studies, to Eastern mysticism, to permaculture and ecological sustainability. For years I had been asking myself the questions: How did we—humanity—get *here*, to this point as a species, and what do we *do* about it? These are precisely the questions that the PCC program seeks to answer, and to which, in some measure, all of its students find themselves compelled. And so I found myself in good company.

~

The following day a group from our online cohort met at the main campus building in the heart of San Francisco's Mission District. This was an opportunity for us to tour the campus, meet with professors, and connect around our unique experience as distance learners. We gathered in a room on the fifth floor (Matt leaned over briefly towards me and whispered conspiratorially that it was *also* the fifth floor that I was on with my brother in

194

my dream…) where, sitting in a circle, we were invited to name and acknowledge our ancestors and guides, those whose influence had brought us to the PCC program at CIIS. I named a list of my spiritual teachers and therapists, those who have supported and helped counsel me through the darkest days of my illness, and whose wisdom has always been a guiding light, as well as the lineages of those who came before and who are no longer with us—stretching back to C.G. Jung, Wilhelm Reich, Paul Brunton, and Plotinus.

At the close of this ceremonial welcoming, we all stood and began the awkward—to me—process of saying our goodbyes. Some rushed off quickly, some lingered and struck-up side conversations with their new professors or classmates, while some exchanged contact information in order to reconnect later. I, myself, stood for a moment in the doorway, awkwardly watching this tableau, wondering if I should go back and try to join in, before resolving, with some chagrin, to simply turn and leave.

My rationale at the time was that these people all lived far from me and thus whatever connections I might make here would likely never last. Nevertheless, I couldn't help but feel a twinge of sadness as I plodded back down the hallway and began to descend the steps to the lobby. A moment later I stepped out onto the busy street, hailed a cab, and was soon tucked into the back seat, watching my new school building shrink in the rear window.

Just then a horrible weight seemed to drop into my stomach, like a void opening up beneath me, and I immediately lamented my decision to leave so abruptly, to not linger, to not say goodbye. This would remain one of my deepest regrets.

That evening I sat on the bed in my airport hotel room and typed out a sheepish message to send to Matt that read only: "I'm sorry I didn't say goodbye."

~

The fall semester ebbed into the spring semester as our studies took us through the links between consciousness and the apparatus of the brain, the history of Western philosophical thought, the cosmological beginnings of the universe, and the evolution of human consciousness. Despite the distance, our classes met regularly over video to create a sense of connection and foment meaningful class discussions. I began to gain my bearings within the community and culture of PCC.[39] I was beginning to discover my voice and find my own thread of inquiry and interest through the wealth of knowledge and philosophical lineage that was being imparted by my professors.

As the spring semester wore on, I looked forward to our next upcoming retreat and my next trip to California. It would be another opportunity to immerse myself in the community, to build relationships with my classmates and professors and engage in esoteric and philosophical discussions the likes of which I couldn't share anywhere else. And it promised a chance to make right what I'd got wrong upon leaving our last retreat.

---

[39] (Matt had joked that once one had grasped the two terms that were required for any philosophy student to know—"ontology" and "epistemology"—it was smooth sailing from there...)

But, as the date drew closer, stress from my personal life had begun to get the better of me and symptoms from my old illness, which had never completely been cured, flared up again. I struggled with the decision, but, in the end, I knew that if I were to make the trip I would feel awful, sick, and miserable the entire time, and wouldn't be able to fully engage with people in the ways that I wanted. And I didn't want my new friends to see me like that, to know me like that. It broke my heart, but I cancelled my trip. I would simply have to wait to attend the next retreat in the fall.

I was particularly sad to have missed seeing Matt again. Since our meeting in the fall I had come to always look forward to his written contributions and presence in class discussions. I do confess that I had developed a bit of a crush on him, as much as was possible across such a distance, and in such a short period of time. I knew that there was nothing to it, and yet my spirits were always buoyed to see him on the other end of my computer video screen.

That week, while my community was gathered in California and I was stuck at home on the couch, I wrote the following passage in response to a class discussion prompt. I include it here because I believe it to be relevant, both to the project and purpose of this book, as well as to what is to come next:

> "[T]he objectification of the divine as separate from nature afforded humanity with a greater sense of freedom to, 'to some extent 'transcend and dominate' the

'limitations imposed by the conditions of . . . existence,'[40] namely suffering. But only 'to some extent,' the limit of which is the ultimate inescapability of death and suffering due to the fact that we all die, everything comes to an end, that is our fate no matter how free or self-aware we may become. This limit to our transcendent capacity for control, coupled with a sense of our tenuous bearings within a dualistically fragmented worldview, leads to a potent anxiety and desire to resist and avoid that which we inevitably must endure. Rather, an ontology of a multicentric immanent divine would offer a powerful balm to the anxiety and trauma of the ultimate lack of control over death and pain/suffering while rendering both, rather, as simply finite perceptive experiences in an otherwise infinite background/reality of divine beingness."

Unbeknownst to me, it was also around this time that Matt had written a similar sentiment:

"The finitude. I spend time and energy worrying about the fact that my physical time will end, and ways to prolong [defer] that reality, but it is the crucible in which we all burn. The tiredness of my existence informs nearly all decisions I make and the creative-ness colors those decisions. Time is on my side. Time waits for no man. No thing so certain as Death. No thing so uncertain as time. Time heals all wounds..."

---

[40] Belah, Robert N. "Religious Evolution." *American Sociological Review*, Vol. 29, No. 3 (Jun., 1964), pp. 358-374; p. 361.

~ To be continued... ~

CHAPTER TWENTY-SEVEN

LIFE ADVICE

Here is my well-considered advice to people in each age group of life.

INFANT TO FOUR YEARS:

> *Imagine what you can.*
> *Believe what you want.*
> *Control your behavior so others don't have to.*

FIVE TO TEN YEARS:

> *Imagine what you can.*
> *Believe what you want.*
> *Control your behavior so others don't have to.*

ELEVEN TO EIGHTEEN YEARS:

> *Imagine what you can.*
> *Believe what you want.*
> *Control your behavior so others don't have to.*

NINETEEN TO THIRTY-FIVE YEARS:

> *Imagine what you can.*
> *Believe what you want.*
> *Control your behavior so others don't have to.*

201

THIRTY-SIX TO FIFTY-FIVE YEARS:

Imagine what you can.
Believe what you want.
Control your behavior so others don't have to.

FIFTY-SIX TO EIGHTY-FIVE YEARS:

Imagine what you can.
Believe what you want.
Control your behavior so others don't have to.

EIGHTY-SIX TO ONE HUNDRED FIFTY YEARS:

Imagine what you can.
Believe what you want.
Control your behavior so others don't have to.

Chapter Twenty-Eight

Encounter with a Dreamer

Part II

I am in the highlands of Scotland in an old house or castle overlooking a small town nestled in the valley at the edge of a loch. It is night and the sky is clear and dark and dotted with stars.

I see my friend Sue making her way through the cobble-stoned alleys towards the town. I run down to meet her. I catch up to her and we are standing now at the shore of the loch, talking.

Suddenly I look up to see a defective satellite hurtling down directly towards me. Sue grabs me and pulls me out of its path just before it crashes down to earth with a thunderous impact—I feel it reverberate through me, as if my very bones have been rattled.

It has landed just where I was standing, half in the water and half on land, where it has crushed a small dinghy that now lies in splinters and pieces. I feel so grateful to Sue for saving my life and am severely rattled by this close-call.

I woke up from this dream on the morning of April 16th, 2019, and immediately reached for my phone. The imagery was too salient—and too like my previous dream of a satellite hurtling to earth—to ignore. I quickly typed out a brief message, under the heading "Hope this isn't annoying, but...": "...I had another dream about a satellite falling from the sky. WTF?! Hope yr well," and sent it to my classmate Matt, the dreamer. I waited in anticipation for his reply, anxious for the opportunity to share my dream with him and discuss the conspicuous parallels to my earlier dream.

A week went by without a response, which was not particularly out of the ordinary—we were, after all, only classmates, not friends, per se—but still, it seemed unlike him to ignore a friendly correspondence, especially one pertaining to dreams. I will admit, I felt sad and a bit hurt by his silence.

Until I discovered why...

On April 15th Matt had driven up to Yosemite National Park for a solo day-hike. He never returned.

What is known, or supposed, about his death is that he was scrambling up a talus slope, either to reach an overlook or on his way back down, when he fell.

The news came through in an email from our graduate program director. I opened it and read—

> *"Dear Friends,*
>
> *I'm saddened to be writing you this afternoon, but we have just learned of the death of Matt Flowers . . ."*

I read it again, not believing, my mind frantically trying to find some way around it—perhaps there was another Matt Flowers...?

But no. The reality of it pierced and clawed at my insides, seeming to wrench them from my guts.

That night I sobbed for a very long while.

~

The following days passed in a haze. I felt empty and exhausted, like the bottom of me had opened up and everything had simply fallen out.

Together, our community mourned and supported one another in our loss, but privately I felt tossed about on waves of rage and grief. Every fiber of my being wanted to rail against reality, against the truth of it. I hated the idea of living in a world in which Matt was no longer living. Most of all I felt bereft that I would never get to talk to him again, or get a chance to know him better, to banter and hear his wise and kind words. I so bitterly regretted not attending the retreat just two weeks before. And not saying goodbye the last—and only—time we had met.

One night, as I was driving home in the dark thinking about Matt, tears streaming down my face, and feeling so frustrated that I couldn't tell him how sad and sorry I was, I realized suddenly—or simply decided—that there was, in fact, no reason why I couldn't. And so when I arrived home I opened my laptop and navigated to the message I had sent him only a week before upon waking from my poignantly synchronous dream, and wrote this message:

"I waited all week for a response, thinking it seemed unlike you to not write back. But when I heard about

your passing, I realized that the dream I had was about you.

See, when my grandmother passed away, I dreamt that I was hit in the back of the head with a frying pan—I woke up so suddenly that I sat straight up in bed. The next morning I learned that she had passed around the same time that I had that dream. And the morning after my best friend's boyfriend nearly died in a car accident (unbeknownst to me) I rolled over and grabbed my phone to call her before I was even awake enough to know what I was doing. Then there was the dream I had about my best friend's girlfriend two days before she died by suicide. Or the time I dreamt that my friend was sick and when I texted him the next day found out that he was in the hospital about to go in for open heart surgery. I so wish I could tell you about all these dreams and more, hear your thoughts and theories, witness your awe and passion for the power of dream and the mysterious unknown.

You were the only one I told that dream to, about the falling satellite at the end of the world, on the car ride to San Francisco last fall . . . And so when I had another dream about a falling satellite last Monday night I woke up and of course thought of you, not knowing that you were already gone. So I think I felt it, on some level. I think something in me knew, and communicated through the image of the satellite falling from the night sky.

I don't know why I should be so sensitive to your death. We met only so briefly. And yet I feel it so deeply, like the wind being knocked out of me every time I think of

206

your face or your voice or your kind eyes, your bright smile, the generosity of your entire being. As soon as I met you, I felt that you were a kindred spirit—and not just in an intellectual PCC way, but on some other level, on a heart and soul level. Listening to your friends and classmates speak about and remember you, as we came together in communion and solidarity over the grief of your passing, I realized that it was not just me: so many of the people who knew you felt that kindred heart and soul connection with you. Because that is how you moved through the world. That is how you met people, with such a generous, loving, and attentive heart-presence. We all felt it. And we all feel the loss of you so deeply.

But for myself, I felt so instantly safe and open with you (a feat for a social recluse like me); you made me feel seen and at ease. To be honest, you were THE person I was most looking forward to seeing at this past Spring Retreat. I'm sorry I didn't make it, I'm so sorry I didn't get the opportunity to reconnect with you and bask in the warmth of your kind friendship one last time. Though it may not make any rational sense—again since I only knew you so briefly—I know that part of me loved you and I know that I will always carry your memory with great fondness in my heart, and I'm so grateful to have met you.

Again I will say, I'm sorry I didn't say goodbye to you after the fall retreat. I knew then that I had made a mistake, I just didn't know how big. We must never take one another for granted, nor the moments we have together on this plain. Thank you for teaching me that.

I don't want to say "rest in peace" because that sounds so boring and not you, so I'll say: Be alive with the atoms and stars, bring each concrescing moment to its fullest, dream the world into being, my brilliant, soulful friend. You are missed and you are loved.

Yours ever,
Meghan"

~

Several days later I marshalled my resolve to resume my studies—it had felt too wrenchingly heartbreaking to consider moving on without Matt, but time ebbs ever onward, and so does homework. It was a bright warm early spring day, and I took my book out into the yard and laid down on my belly on the soft new grass under a still bare pear tree, and opened to a new page.

Still, the grief washed over me and I lay my head down on the pages of the open book. I felt the solidity of the soft earth beneath me, of the tender press of gravity holding us together; I felt the warmth of the sun on my back and the sharp tickle of the grass on my skin; I heard the birds chirping their songs in the trees around me and the gentle scuff of my farm animals grazing nearby—the pigs enjoying the spring sun on the bellies and the cows munching languidly in their pastures. Everything felt so familiarly solid and enduring.

But then, suddenly, that solidity seemed to burst open into a tremendous sense of permeability. I felt the world instead as a shimmering porous lightness made of myriad bubbles simply floating and popping, while the real enduring solidity was, in truth, just on the other side of all this materiality. In that moment I felt I could glimpse through the mirage of this world to the oasis beyond—or within.

And there was Matt. Just there. I felt his warm smiling presence, his playful joyousness, his sincere steadfast attention. It was as if I, lying there, the weight of my body held against the earth, were instead pressed against the thinnest film of glass, just on the other side of which stood Matt, also pressed this close. I let myself sink into this sensation, into the comfort of this knowing, let it reverberate through my whole being. And in that instant I was changed by it; my life was irrevocably altered.

~

Knowing, as I do now, that he was always just right there—right here, as it were—I continued talking and writing to Matt over the ensuing months. I still do, sometimes. Mostly I would write to him about my dreams.

"Dear Matt, are you there? The last two nights I've dreamt about..."

"Dear Matt, I dreamt again, last night, of something falling violently from the sky..."

"Dear Matt, my dreams last night were so vivid!..."

"Hi Matt, last night I remember dreaming about traveling..."

I would also sometimes—not always with words, but with my heart—ask him for help, for his guidance. When I would lie awake in the dark of the night seething with the angst and agita of my fragile, insecure human ego, I remembered him and that day lying in the grass and I would call upon him for his assistance, for his soothing comfort, for his compassion and forgiveness when I could not muster it for myself. And I found that he was always—always—there. Sometimes even in comically serendipitous ways...

~

Six and a half months after his death our PCC community once again gathered together in California, this time at the famed Esalen Institute in Big Sur. Esalen has been a center of spiritual retreat and esoteric studies for more than half a century, and sits perched upon the cliff's edge over-looking the vast expanse of the Pacific Ocean. As such it elicits the visceral experience of a powerful enclave nestled against the Redwood studded Santa Lucia Mountains. At Esalen one feels pressed upon all sides— the imposing mountains to the one side, the forbidding Pacific to the other. One can practically feel the earth turning underneath one's feet as the sun sets into the distant ocean horizon, and the experience is almost dizzying, causing one's stomach to lurch disconcertingly as if one is clinging madly to the earth lest one be spun off, either down into the commanding depths of the ocean or perhaps out into the vacuum of space.

Or at least that's how it felt to a lifetime East-coaster like myself. Regardless, the effect arouses a sense of intense psychic pressure, like entering a sacred chamber or alembic in which the veil is thin between the seen and unseen realms, the *tonal y nagual*, and all who enter may be propelled—or sometimes

210

catapulted—into or through a deeply transformative process. Simply put, there is an air of magic about the place.

It was a wonderful week spent in deep and playful conversation and heartfelt connections; powerful and absorbing lectures and presentations made by our colleagues and friends; hikes among the impressive Redwoods still scorched from fires passed; nourishing relaxation in the hot-spring baths; moments of private contemplation and revelry in the beauty and wonder of the place; and the privilege of being a part of such a vibrant, caring, and not just highly educated, but truly wise community. And all the time we were there I was aware of Matt's absence and how much he would have loved to be with us all in this beautiful and sacred environment.

And he was, of course. We evoked him throughout the week, in photos and memories shared, and in bittersweet moments of homage over a glass of beer or wine at the end of a full day.

On our last night together, I wrote to him:

"Hi Matt,

I'm here—we're all here—at Esalen, missing you. It's hard to put into words all that this experience has been. It's been a rollercoaster of thoughts and emotions; it's been a challenge and a joy; it's been...very full.

I really wish you were here. But/And I recognize that— as others have said—the sacrifice of your death was and continues to be in service to all of us. I know it has been for me—a potent teacher in my own process of awakening over these past six months. I have so much gratitude for you, in life and in death.

211

And, also, I really wish you were here in body, to talk to and listen and laugh with—you would have loved the hike into the canyon today.

Be well, my friend."

The next day at the airport with my classmate and friend, Emily—who had also known and loved Matt—we found a private little alcove between an escalator and a wide window, hidden behind a large column, away from the bustle of travelers rushing to and fro'. We tucked our bags aside and settled down on a bench in this out-of-the-way place to wait until the very last minute before we had to say our goodbyes and go our separate ways.

For some reason, perhaps anticipating a quiet moment to jot down some thoughts, I had pulled my journal from my bag and sat with it in my lap. Suddenly, with no particular purpose, I opened the book to the above note and began to read out loud: "Hi Matt…" I said.

Just at that moment a man, likely spying a clear route free from foot traffic in the alley between the escalator and the windows, passed-by in front of us. He started at my voice, as I was discretely hidden behind the large column, and he stopped and turned to look expectantly at me and Emily. I laughed awkwardly, gesturing towards the book to explain that I had just been reading aloud, and apologized for startling him.

He nodded in bemused comprehension and replied, "my name *is* Matt, though." We all laughed at the coincidence before he rushed off into the fray.

After he had gone Emily and I just looked at one another and smiled in wonder at this puckish synchronicity.

"Hi Matt," I repeated once more, this time in recognition.

~

The veil is ever so thin. We mistake it for a hard and hopelessly, heartlessly impenetrable barrier. When we come upon it in that moment between when someone is here with us and when they are inexplicably gone—for death is always inexplicable, no matter the circumstances—we rail against it. We throw our bodies, our hearts, nay, our whole beings against it like the ramparts of some formidable fortress, and are rebuffed time and time again. The harder we flail the more painful, more rigidly unyielding, and more cruelly impervious this barrier seems.

But it is not. It is only—which is to say "simply," though certainly not "merely," for the distinction is poignantly tragic— a matter of perception. We cannot see what our eyes cannot see; we cannot hear what our ears cannot hear; we cannot touch what our skin cannot sense; we cannot hold what our arms cannot enfold within them. And yet we can still *feel* beyond only what we can see, hear, touch, and hold. We can loosen and widen our perception to that which lies beyond this. Though it does not change the longing for the solid, for the sensual, for the personally precious. It does not render that which cannot be replaced any less priceless and worthy of our most conscientious protection.

It is an act of faith—of *trust*—to lean into what cannot be seen or touched. It is an act of trust to whisper into the darkness and it is an act of trust to listen, in open and earnest sincerity, for a reply. Allowing oneself to fall into and be held by the vital immanence—that buoyant porous shimmering effervescence—one finds a permeating lightness and a deep comfort, in contrast to the harsh finite solidity encountered by our physical senses alone. It is, perhaps, an experience of in-*spir*-ation, of the exhilarating dynamic vibrancy, of love in its truest form.

When we love someone, each other, this world, our own irreplaceable lives, so intensely, we are sure that without them life itself becomes more empty, dreary, meaningless, and oppressive. We are sure that death is an evil with which we are constantly plagued, always standing, as we are, on the precipice of utter calamity and disaster. The fear of it oppresses us, grips us, holds us fast to the fleeting pleasures and pains of this finite little life to which we so desperately cling. So long as it is all we know—all we *allow* ourselves to know—we remain prisoner to that constant burden: the knowledge that someday we all—and indeed all of this precious world, all that we hold most dear—must pass away.

But, again, we mistake the object for the substance, the effect for the cause, the thing for its source. We think that the ones we love, the world we love, this life that we love, are the source of our experience *of* love, this feeling that fills us to bursting with pleasure and joy. But they are not the source of our love, they are simply the pale and flimsy dressings of love. None of us, nor this world, are objects of love. Rather, love is *what we are*, not what we have to give. This goes for everything—all is but the veil that love wears.

214

Every facet of this manifest universe is veil. Our finite physical existences, our bodies, and all the bodies of the manifest world—trees and cars, oxygen and water, cancer cells and assault rifles—all are simply threads of the veil; our passing pleasures and pains are veil; our thoughts, images, dreams, judgments and opinions: all veil; our feelings—shame, rage, fear: veil; our histories and government systems: veil; money and the economy: veil; hierarchies: veil; white supremacy, cisheteropatriarchy, xenophobic imperialist greed: veil, veil, veil veil veil; right or wrong: veil; our conceptions of good and evil: veil; hatred: veil; even what we so often like to think of and exalt as love is merely veil, a pale and flimsy facsimile of the true phenomenon.

Because love is not a personal thing. It is not to be conferred on one person or another, on one place or another, on one thing or another, and it is never to be conditional—it cannot pass away but endures eternally. Rather, it is like a wind that blows through us, filling us like a sail—it is love which animates and brings us to life. And it is love that welcomes us home upon our return in death.

Indeed, if the whole world were to disappear, cease to exist, burn up in a fiery nuclear explosion, only the veil would be snatched away; the love would ever remain.

Again, this does not mean that all the threads and ripples of the veil are not worth fighting for, nor that its more destructive aspects are not worth fighting against. Just because they aren't the whole truth doesn't mean they aren't real. Or, as William Douglas Horden likes to say, "a mirage is a real thing—it's just not what it looks like." The truth of this world, of this universe,

215

is more and deeper and greater than our senses would have us believe, but that does not mean that what we can sense is meaningless and unimportant. When presented with the finest silk scarf, do we not thumb it preciously? Do we not relish its exquisite texture? If it smells lightly of roses, do we not savor the scent?

Matt taught—and indeed continues, to teach me this: to let myself trust, to let myself relax and surrender into the loving embrace of the immanent beyond, of the *nagual*, that is always just right here. And it is remembering this, it is *feeling* this—deeply, to the very core of my being—that makes living in a time of dying, such as this, not quite so ominous and frightening; it is this which gives me the courage and the grace, and even—or perhaps especially—the joy to carry on.

> *"If this is the cosmic dream,*
> *then we have all been created effortlessly,*
> *to keep the dream going."*
>
> ~ *Matt Flowers*[41]

---

[41] Quote from Matt's "Lucid Dreaming Mandala" presentation given on April 3rd, 2019 at the PCC spring, not two weeks before his death, which can be viewed at:
https://www.youtube.com/watch?v=k-zWqavXDRU&feature=youtu.be.

CONCLUSION

But, you may still be asking, how *do* we *live*, how do we continue to move forward, in such a time of incomprehensible dying? How can we face the devastation and despair wrought not only by a global pandemic, human-made ecological collapse, and a mounting sixth mass extinction, but by *our own continued* destructive actions and cynical indifference? How is one to face the demise of all that one holds most precious and dear?

First of all, dear friends, we must *feel* it. All the grief, all the rage, all the sadness, all the *love* that fills one to bursting, or perhaps even breaking. It is in feeling our grief that we pay homage to what has been and is being lost; it is in feeling our rage that we summon the power to protect that which is most vulnerable; it is in feeling our sadness that we soften our hearts to the world; and it is in feeling our love that we know *why* and *what is at stake*.

In order to remain true to our feelings we must continually check in with our bodies, those instruments of physical resonance; with our hearts, that ever open and inviting threshold to empathic knowing; with our spirits, the immanent divine within each of us that guides us ever towards our own pinnacle of fulfillment; and with our integrity, the vital wisdom of our whole beings.

We must devote ourselves to making intentional choices in every thought, word, and deed as we participate in the co-creative unfolding of the universe and this, our world.

We must commit ourselves to connecting deeply and authentically with others in nourishing and joyful community, as well as in respectful and deliberate fellowship and solidarity across all arbitrary borders and boundaries. This means both supporting the needs of others when we can, as well as submitting to lean-in to those who have the capacity to support and nourish us when we're scared or sad, or simply feel too broken by the brokenness of the world to hold ourselves up in that moment.[42]

In just such moments, we must also be willing to hold ourselves and one another with compassion and forgiveness as we muddle through, not only the enigmatic terrain of our own emotional landscapes and wounded psyches, but also through the impossibly convoluted and inhumane challenges of living under, and through, the mind-numbing, heart-dulling, spirit-breaking, traumatizing, and alienating divisiveness and exploitation of this modern "civilization," or *colon*ization.

And we must ground ourselves, our bodies, hearts, minds, and spirits, with the *courage to love* what is dying.

> "To *live* in this world,
> You must be willing to do three things:
> To *love* what is mortal;
> To hold it against your bones

---

[42] Hint: normalize going to therapy and decolonize therapy!

Knowing your *own life* depends on it;
And when the time comes
To let it go,
To *let it go.*"[43]

To live in this world, we must contend with its dying. More than that, we must learn to love it *for* its dying. Because it is in the embrace of dying, by leaning *in* to the yawning abyss of dying, of the *nagual*, that we may really and truly cherish our living. And *that* is what living is for; that is what is being asked of us, every one—that we *cherish* our living, that we *love* what it is to be mortal, that we *revel* in the *pure enjoyment* of this existence *for its own sake*.

When faced with such senseless, incomprehensible, heart-rending pain we must endeavor, in every way and with all manner of grace, to make it *matter*, to make it *significant*, to make it *sacred*. Because when we make of this world a garden where everything is meaningful and sacred, even death, then dying itself is not the end of living, but simply another vestige of this generous, dynamic, vibrant, beautiful, and ever-beloved thing called living.

---

[43] Gratitude again to the great Mary Oliver for these words from her poem "In Blackwater Woods"; italics added for emphasis.

221

EPILOGUE

Life is tragic simply because the earth turns and the sun inexorably rises and sets, and one day, for each of us, the sun will go down for the last, last time. Perhaps the whole root of our trouble, the human trouble, is that we will sacrifice all the beauty of our lives, will imprison ourselves in totems, taboos, crosses, blood sacrifices, steeples, mosques, races, armies, flags, nations, in order to deny the fact of death, which is the only fact we have...

~ James Baldwin,
The Fire Next Time

We, particularly in Western culture, have a fear of death. We fear its incomprehensible impenetrable permanence; we fear the unknown beyond this life, this world, this universe that we can touch and see and feel.

We fear this unknown because we have come to believe that it is either simply a vast nothing, a coldly indifferent nonexistence, or else it is something somewhere far away from here, from all that we know and love and cherish in this world.

We did not always believe this. In fact, it is a fairly recent development, considering the vast history of human existence. And, thankfully, there are many still who remember, who have not forgotten, and who maintain a connection, a vital relationship, to the realm of what we call the dead, the land of the beyond.

The indigenous Nahuatl peoples of what is now considered Mexico and the southwestern United States call this realm the *nagual*, the hidden realm. The *nagual* is the land of the soul. Here in the *tonal*, the realm of what we call life, the soul is a visitor, a tourist—it delights in every moment of manifest existence. But in the *nagual* the soul is at home.

The *nagual y tonal* entwine together like lovers. Like the two halves of the taijitu—the yin-yang symbol—they require one another for their own existence and perpetually lean and turn into one another in a kaleidoscope of being and becoming, or what we call living and dying.

From here in the *tonal* the *nagual* is always just this close, differentiated only by the thinnest of veils. In truth, we can *touch* it, we can *see* it, we can *feel* it, though perhaps not in the ways that we are used to from the vantage point and with the sensory apparatuses available in the *tonal*. We have only forgotten how.

And we have only to remember.

But our forgetting has caused us great pain and fear. It is the pain and fear of believing that we are separate, that we have been abandoned to this fragmented and finite world, to a fragmented and finite existence, at the end of which lies only the finality of death. We find ourselves naked and afraid and so terribly terribly alone.

And so we *fight* by fang and claw to cling to whatever fragile finite security we can grasp within this thing called living;

And so we *flee* from the unknown—from the perilous "other"—lest we be consumed by it;

And so we *freeze* ourselves against our own vulnerability.

But in so doing we unwittingly wage war against our own blood, against those who would be our soul companions both here and beyond; we unwittingly desert our own hearts and eschew the relational bonds that have sustained us for millennia; and we unwittingly numb ourselves to *feeling* and paralyze the dynamic vitality of the life force that is our birthright.

This is the trauma wrought from a belief in a separateness which divides us, and in the finitude of life. This is the consequence of our fear of death. It has compelled us to do unspeakable things in the name of security, of so-called "safety," and, ultimately, of control.

Perhaps we have forgotten how to *touch*, *see*, and *feel* into the unknown because our rituals have been stolen from us. Our sacred indigenous rites of communion with the *nagual* were, at various times, and by brutal violence, forbidden to us, denigrated as pagan heresy and "savage" superstition.

Those who maintain their connection with the other half of existence have done and continue to do so at great peril and with great courage. Their struggle is for all of us. They have been remembering for all of us.

It is time for us to take up this charge again. It is time for us to reclaim our *knowing* of, our *feeling* with, and our *belonging* to the whole of existence. We deserve more than this half-life. We *are* more than this half-life would have us believe.

If we are to truly survive—not only physically, but spiritually and emotionally, as whole beings within a whole community within a whole world—then we must embrace our dying. We must fall into it with open arms and an open heart, vulnerable and soft to its tender caresses, as it welcomes us to the home which, in truth, we never left.

> *...It seems to me that one ought to rejoice in the <u>fact</u> of death—ought to decide, indeed, to <u>earn</u> one's death by confronting with passion the conundrum of life. One is responsible to life: it is the small beacon in that terrifying darkness from which we come and to which we shall return. One must negotiate this passage as nobly as possible, for the sake of those who are coming after us.*
>
> ~ James Baldwin,
> *The Fire Next Time*

228

APPENDIX I

LIVING IN A TIME OF DYING:

AN ASTROLOGICAL PERSPECTIVE

By Meghan Elizabeth Tauck

It was in the fall of 2016, not two weeks before that fateful presidential election, when I first noticed it coming: the Saturn-Pluto conjunction of 2020. I took particular notice of this impending astrological signature because it promised to be of significant import to me personally, as it implicated several major signatures in my own natal chart. But astrologers across the globe had also trained their eyes on this momentous aspect, watching, waiting, and, yes, hypothesizing what might come to pass...

At the time I had been studying astrology for about ten years and had learned to decipher the archaic symbols for the constellations and planets, their archetypal signatures, and the latter's movements against the cosmic backdrop. For the uninitiated, astrology is the oldest—literally the first—science, elucidating knowledge, foresight, and meaning from the geocentric observation of the movement of the other planets in our solar system against the backdrop of the twelve ecliptic constellations.

For thousands of years—even, literally, since before we were human—we have looked up at the sky and organized our lives around the movements of celestial phenomena, perhaps first the great luminaries, the Sun and Moon, and later the "wandering" stars, which we now understand to be the visible planets of Mercury, Venus, Mars, Jupiter, and Saturn. Across the globe and across all cultures, people have drawn intelligence and meaning from the travels and meetings of these cosmic beings. It is from these thousands of years of observation and meaning-making, as well as the important later discoveries of the invisible bodies of Uranus, Neptune, Pluto, the asteroid field, and now Eris, that we have come to our current understanding and practice of astrology.

In the practice of natal astrology, one calculates a chart of where the luminaries, planetary bodies, and asteroids were, relative to the place on earth where an individual was born, and at the precise time of their birth. The signatures of the luminary and planetary archetypes against the backdrop of the twelve constellations and in relationship (called "aspect") to one another, elucidate significant meaning about the life and personality of the individual. Then, as the celestial bodies continue their dancing rotations around the ecliptic they continue to interact (*aspect*), both with each other and with the placements in an individual's chart (called "transits"). Such *transits* have both collective significance (as, for example, when the Sun enters Cancer everyone the world over experiences the hemispheric season associated with the Sun being in Cancer) and private import and expression for the individual (as, for example, during the infamous "Saturn return").

230

To the Cartesian-Newtonian Western mind, raised to believe that all matter is simply inert "stuff" thrown into motion by invisible forces like gravity, or even the "hand of God," such claims of astrological significance and consequence may sound absurd. How could planets so far from us, with no scientifically, physically measurable force acting upon earth (such as the gravitational pull of the Moon) have anything to do with what happens on earth, much less the inner psychology and personal development of every individual person?

I am aware of the skeptical arguments, and my response to them is twofold: Firstly, I refer to quantum physics[44] and the process-relational ontology of mathematician and philosopher Alfred North Whitehead, who, in his magnum opus, *Process and Reality*,[45] offers a stunning metaphysical scheme articulating the interconnection and interdependence of literally all things in existence. A sufficient treatment of his work, however, would outpace the purview of this book. Suffice it to say that just because we cannot scientifically measure with our physical apparatus the influence of the stars and planets on human existence, does not mean that it isn't real and true. To that end, I refer also to Carl Gustav Jung's theory of synchronicity, which, he writes,

> "takes the coincidence of events in space and time as meaning something more than mere chance, namely, a peculiar *interdependence* of objective events among

---

[44] Consider the implication of quantum entanglement...
[45] Free Press: New York, 1978 [1929].

themselves as well as with the subjective (psychic) states of the observer."[46]

In other words, there is a subtle but nevertheless *participatory* relationship between the objective external, physical world of events in space-time and the subjective internal, metaphysical realm of experience. Thus, the movement of the planets against the backdrop of stars participates synchronistically with life on earth just as we participate with the planets through our own conscious meaning-making processes. This constant and eternal intercourse between the mundane and the mysterious, between the fallaciously dichotomized matter and spirit, between finite human awareness and the infinitely Universal One Mind, is what makes astrology—and, for that matter, any other form of divination, magic, ritual, or prayer—in a word: significant. By interacting with and/or simply observing the materia of nature and of the universe, we are necessarily in communication with it, with the divine.

For example, if the import and power of astrological significations had not already become clear to me, it might have done so in the years 2011-2016. It was during those years that Uranus, the god of freedom and rebellion, and Pluto, the god of transformation and the death-rebirth cycle, danced in a *square* (90°) aspect to one another, back and forth in retrograde and direct motion. This was their first square aspect since they were together in the sky (*conjunction*) in the mid to late 1960s, when the world erupted with the revolutionary spirit of the psychedelic, free love, feminist, anti-war, and civil rights

---

[46] Wilhelm, Richard & Baynes, Cary F. *The I Ching: Book of Changes.* Princeton University Press: Princeton, NJ, 1977, p. xxiv.

movements, additionally spurring the later Black Power, gay rights, and American Indian movements, which signaled a death of the status quo and a rebirth of a newly transformed awareness of "the power of the people." Again, in 2011 through 2014, we saw revolutionary movements spread like wildfire across the middle east and North Africa in a similar uprising of an emancipatory democratic "people power" in what is known as the Arab Spring.

But revolution is a messy business, whether personal or collective, as it involves the breakdown and overthrow of a prior order before a new one can arise. Thus, it is often a time of great tension, conflict, chaos, and uncertainty, which can be just as devastating when experienced within the personal life and psyche as in the collective world at large.

In addition to world events during these tumultuous years, I personally witnessed and experienced a powerful sense of uncertainty and grief in the wake of this period, with what seemed to be an almost mass exodus of dear souls from our planet, passing away suddenly and without warning, signaling a different kind of emancipatory "uprising" from the physical plain in literal death.

It is important to note that astrology does not suggest that events on earth, nor life experiences or psychological complexes within the individual psyche, are fatalistically *caused* by the placements of the planetary bodies. Rather, what astrology offers is a kind of archetypal time-piece for myriad phenomena. Whereas a clock simply shows us the time of day based on the movement of the Sun relative to earth, the astrological zodiac tells us the "time" based on the archetypal signatures and *meanings* of the planetary bodies which have been elucidated over hundreds and indeed thousands of years. Thus, just as we know that the Sun nearing the western horizon signifies that night is coming, so the angles of the planets in relation to one another signify the advent of certain archetypal signatures.

An *archetype* is a kind of representative or symbolic idea or ideal of a lived experience. Rather than being static, monolithic, or definitive, archetypes offer a fluid and infinite wealth of meanings. In the same way that "a picture is worth a thousand words," an archetype speaks volumes about the "thing" which it represents. Thus, the archetype of Uranus, the god of freedom and rebellion, could include a host of significators, from the violent overthrow of governments to the breakthrough of sudden enlightenment to the freedom of expression in a new style or haircut. Its significance runs the gamut, from the extreme to the minute, and from the personal/internal/psychic to the collective/external/social. Similarly, Pluto, the god of transformation and the death-rebirth cycle, may bring us to profound psycho-spiritual encounters with our own deepest latent fears and desires, or expose feelings of powerlessness in the face of the greater forces of nature, including that of death itself, whether of the physical body or of deeply entrenched complexes of the psyche, or it may herald seismic shifts in the social fabric through the overturning of old systems and the institution of new modes of power and human relationship.

An archetype is never prescriptive, only *de*scriptive. But we can use our understanding of the planetary archetypes to *choose* how we will prepare for, respond to, and align ourselves with their archetypal imperatives, just as we would approaching the close of day at sunset. This is the imperative distinction between

234

futility and freedom, between resigning oneself to some fatalistic determinism of what *will* be versus accepting one's participatory agency to affect what *can* be. The power and potential in astrology is not simply to dictate what must happen, but to afford us a language of meaning with which to co-creatively participate with the progressive unfolding of the universe. It is this language of archetypes that helps us to understand and thus agentically respond to the exigencies of the times.

Now, Saturn and Pluto both have rather infamous reputations in astrology. The Pluto archetype represents continual change and renewal; it overturns everything we thought we knew, everything we thought we could rely on, in its never-ending imperative to transform the old and familiar into the new and as yet to be determined. Pluto marks the threshold between the known and unknown, between this world and the mysterious beyond, between living and dying, and as such can usher in periods of profound dissolution and transformation. For this reason, Pluto periods can be quite disorienting and frightening, even as they inevitably propel us—albeit sometimes kicking and screaming—forward in our own personal as well as collective social evolution. Pluto turns our world upside-down. Everything we thought we knew is tossed up in the air under Pluto signatures, and we are left, for a time, suspended in the discomfort and anxiety of not knowing, before finding our feet again on new terrain, with a new perspective of the world, and ourselves.

Meanwhile, the archetype of Saturn calls us to take responsibility, to dedicate ourselves to something and stand in our own integrity, which necessarily means that we must limit our options and erect some boundaries within our lives—around our time, our relationships, and our bodies—in order to focus on our task at hand, what we are called to do and become. One cannot be all things at all times; eventually one must choose a path, choose a vocation, choose where to take a stand in history and the world. And that means leaving behind other possibilities and erstwhile freedoms. As such, Saturn requires constriction and deprivation. It squeezes us into a form; it is the pressure of time that transforms coal into diamonds.

If we don't nurture and cultivate the Saturn archetype within ourselves over the course of our lives as the intention and dedication to the development of our own inner source of integrity, then we inevitably encounter the archetypal Saturn from the outside, as oppressive authority figures or by social or institutional mechanisms. When we are too young to stand on our own, our parents or guardians (hopefully) play the role of Saturn, helping us to build that internal structure so that as we age we are equipped with the necessary boundaries, fortitude, and self-control to survive and thrive on our own in the big wide world. However, if we aren't able, for whatever reason, to develop our inner Saturn, at some point we will experience the big wide world as a crushing weight. Saturn is weight, gravitas: either we own it, or it owns us.

Together, over the centuries, as Saturn and Pluto have circled one another, they have marked times of intense suffering, but also deep collective transformation. Philosopher, historian, and astrologer, Richard Tarnas writes,

> "[T]he successive quadrature [i.e. *conjunction*, *opposition*, and *square*] alignments of the Saturn-Pluto

cycle [have] coincided with especially challenging historical periods marked by a pervasive quality of intense *contraction*: eras of international crisis and conflict, empowerment of reactionary forces and totalitarian impulses, organized violence and oppression, all sometimes marked by lasting traumatic effects. An atmosphere of gravity and tension tended to accompany these three-to-four year periods, as did a widespread sense of epochal closure: 'the end of an era' . . . Profound transformation was a dominant theme . . . through contraction, conservative reaction, crisis and termination."[47]

In the last century these eras have included both the First (*conjunction*) and Second (*square*) World Wars; the beginning of the Cold War in the aftermath of WWII (*conjunction*); the introduction of neoliberal Reaganomics (*conjunction*), which undermined New Deal era economic policies and seeded what has now become rampant economic inequality; as well as the 9/11 World Trade Center attacks in 2001 (*opposition*), ushering in the global "War on Terror" and the United States' ongoing wars with Iraq and Afghanistan in the Middle East. Each of these fundamentally changed the world—including the very means by which we wage war, as well as civil, economic, and international social relations—as we knew it.

Strong Pluto-Saturn signatures were also in effect at the times of each of the crusades, with conjunctions marking the Children's crusade of 1212 as well as the Mongol invasion of China led by

---

[47] Tarnas, Richard. *Cosmos and Psyche: Intimations of a New World View.* Viking: New York, NY, 2006, p. 209.

Genghis Khan, the spread of the Black Plague in the mid-14th century, both the beginning and the end of the Thirty Years' War (Saturn-Pluto have a roughly 30 year cycle) in the 17th century, the publication of *The Communist Manifesto* and the rise of workers rebellions in Europe, as well as the rise of abolitionism in the United States in the mid-19th century, and the advent of the First World War and Cold War in the early and mid-20th century. All of these periods had significant and lasting impacts on the world of the times, marked as they were by the challenges and suffering that often come with conflicts and transitions of power.

The Saturn-Pluto conjunction of 2020 marks another such period of intense conflict, crisis, suffering, and change. Astrologers have been waiting and watching for what this period would hail, given our understanding of the archetypes of both planets and the events with which their conjunctions have coincided in the past. Thus, it is perhaps no surprise that I would anticipate this particular archetypal signature with a good dose of trepidation.

Over the last several years, as Saturn has drawn closer to Pluto, we have collectively experienced what feels like an increasing frenzy and chaos, whether politically, socially, or environmentally, as the foundations of old orders and power structures began to tremble and sway. Politically, the vote for England to exit the European Union—colloquially known as Brexit—rocked the economic and social fabric of Europe, while in the United States impeachment proceedings against a sitting president for possible corruption and conspiracy to interfere with a U.S. election threw into question the integrity of U.S. democracy and influence; socially, in Hong Kong months of massive protests against Chinese hegemony inspired liberatory protests movements the world over, including the Black Lives Matter/Movement for Black Lives that was started in the United States but has spread with supporters all over the world; and environmentally, we have all witnessed the increasing frequency and strength of storms, droughts, floods, and wildfires, as well as record breaking temperatures, on every continent on the planet, causing insecurity of our most fundamental needs of food, water, and housing.

It is important to note that aspect signatures between planets do not simply happen all at once; rather, they ride a bell-curve as they wax and wane over a period of time. The farther and thus slower moving planets, like Saturn and Pluto, have a longer bell-curve than the closer and faster moving planets, like Mercury, Venus, or the Moon, as they draw closer into exact aspect to one another and then pull apart again, often compounding over several weeks to months, sometimes with a retrograde cycle in the mix. Moreover, these signatures can be further influenced by any other planets that might be in aspect with them at the same time.

Herein lies the particular alchemy of the year 2020, because in addition to Saturn's conjunction to Pluto, Jupiter—the archetype of inflation and abundance—conspicuously conjuncted them both at the same time over the course of the entire year, thus enlarging their archetypal signatures—of radical transformation of established structures—with its own pension for excess. Additionally, Mars—the archetype of *inflam*mation, aggravation, and conflict—conjuncted Saturn-Pluto-Jupiter in the beginning of 2020 and then squared them in the summer and again in the late fall, thus adding an incendiary influence to an already challenging and precarious signature.

239

The exact conjunction of Saturn and Pluto occurred January 12-13th, 2020. In the weeks prior, the United States shocked the world by assassinating a top Iranian government official, Qasem Soleimani, instigating an international crisis that many feared could lead to a global conflict the likes of World War III. In retaliation, Iran bombed a military base in Iraq and shot down a Ukrainian passenger flight which they apparently mistook for enemy aircraft. Meanwhile, massive wildfires raged across Australia and news of a mysterious new disease spreading in China had begun percolating through the news. It was a tense couple of weeks that seemed to have us all on the edge of our seats. World War III, thankfully, did not come to pass, and eventually the fires raging in the Outback subsided. Astrologers everywhere seemed to heave a sigh of relief.

Yet it would be another several weeks before the entire world would enter the convulsions of the Covid-19 pandemic.

No one, barring extraordinary psychic abilities, can know what's going to happen in the future. That is the dynamism of archetypes: their representations can take many shapes and forms. The archetypal signature of Saturn-Pluto is, again, the quaking of established power structures and the seed-sowing of new potential order—the death of the old precipitating a rebirth of something new. A global pandemic is certainly one way that such change can manifest, as it did in the cases of the Black Plague of the 14th century and the Spanish Flu of the last century, and as now.

Those who lived through the Covid-19 pandemic will remember how every aspect of life—social, religious, economic, political—was upended (Pluto) and became severely constricted

(Saturn), from closed borders and travel restrictions, to economic depression and austerity, to "social distancing" and fear of transmission. We were all left suspended in the uncertainty of when this nightmare would end, what social, economic, and political upheavals would transpire in the interim, and who we would all be on the other side.

The additional archetypal influences of Jupiter's expansive excess as well as Mars' incendiary volatility indicate the extreme virulence of both the virus as well as popular temperaments within the collective zeitgeist. Thus amid a global lockdown (Pluto-Saturn) in response to a perniciously proliferating (Jupiter) disease, we simultaneously bore witness to explosive (Mars) protest movements, from the global Black Lives Matter phenomenon of the summer of 2020, to the related End SARS movement in Nigeria, to workers strikes in countries across the globe in response to economic inequalities further compounded by unsafe working conditions during the pandemic, to the regrettable but predictable anti-lockdown protests in parts of Europe and the U.S.

One other important aspect of the Plutonian archetype is that of shadow illumination. When something is turned over it necessarily reveals its underbelly, the parts that have been kept hidden. The global Covid-19 pandemic revealed in stark relief the seedy underbellies of our society's unjust power structures, perhaps none so glaringly as in the United States where decades of neoliberal and neoconservative anti-socialist free-market economic policies have created rampant economic inequalities, gutted social protections like health care, and built history's largest incarcerated population, all of which proved disastrous in the wake of Covid-19.

People who could not afford to not work could not lockdown or socially distance without risking going hungry or homeless, such that those who disproportionately bore the brunt of this pandemic were those forced to work on the "frontlines" in lower paying jobs like agricultural growers, food distribution and grocery workers, slaughterhouse and warehouse workers, postal workers, nurses and health care administrators, and teachers. In the U.S., these are also the same people who are more likely to be uninsured and lack access to affordable health care options and thus are more likely to avoid seeking medical assistance if they do become ill, or risk bankruptcy due to exorbitant medical bills. They are also the most likely to have preexisting and often untreated comorbidities, like asthma, heart disease, diabetes, and obesity, which can complicate and increase the fatality of Covid-19.

And, of course, due to 250 years of genocidal policies against Indigenous Americans, 150 years of anti-Black economic policies like Jim Crow, redlining, and mass incarceration, a century of neocolonial policies in the South and Central Americas, and four decades of neoliberal trickle-down economic policies at home, these workers are more likely to be poor, immigrants, Indigenous, and/or Black.

Native Americans, who now make up only 2% of the American population,[48] contracted Covid-19 at 3.5 times the rate of white Americans, according to the Centers for Disease Control and Prevention.[49] It is widely known that Black, Indigenous, and

---

[48] (which, it bears stating, is a *98% decrease* in population since first contact with Europeans).
[49] *Weekly* / August 28, 2020 / 69(34);1166–1169.

Latine communities experienced significantly higher rates of death to Covid-19. And as of December 2020, 20% of those incarcerated in the U.S. had contracted Covid-19, a population that is disproportionately Black and Latine, compared to 5% of the general population.[50]

Simply put, the Covid-19 pandemic has laid bare social inequities and injustices that have existed as entrenched in the framework of the status quo, allowing certain others to get ahead and enjoy social and economic privileges and protections that others are not privy to, and which threaten the safety and security of all when faced with a virus that cares not for our superficial and arbitrary differences and demarcations. As we have discovered, we are only as secure as the least secure among us.

Herein lies the genius—yes, genius—of this big little virus: it illuminated for all the world to see how arbitrary and transgressable are our myriad borders, be they national or social, and how interdependent we truly are. For all our differences, we are yet one people, and we survive, or die, together.

The Covid-19 pandemic is only one—only the most recent—of such indicators: the climate crisis that we find ourselves solidly within—no longer looming "out there" somewhere in the nebulous future—is a far greater and no less urgent threat to our collective survival. Perhaps—hopefully—the global effort in containing the Covid-19 pandemic might prove to be a practice round for a much larger collective marshalling of our best capacities and cooperative intentions as a species to help stem

---

[50] According to a report by Beth Schwartzapfel, Katie Park, and Andrew Demillo in The Marshall Project.org, December 18, 2020.

the tide of the climate chaos that our industries and capitalist affluence have created.

And this is where I begin to turn and look to the future…

~

The planets never stop their circling; their cycles only build one onto the other in a kind of fractal cosmic evolutionary dance continuing for as long as the mind can fathom. The Saturn-Pluto conjunction of 2020 is only one such conjunction amid an endless series of cyclical Saturn-Pluto aspect signatures, which is itself only one among the myriad cyclical aspect signatures of all the planets combined. Altogether they weave an ever-evolving fractal tapestry of archetypal relationships and significance spanning the course of time.

The Saturn-Pluto conjunction of 2020, after making a noticeable shift in mid-December of that year, will wane over the course of 2021 as Saturn pulls away from the much slower Pluto. Over the ensuing years, we will witness the germination and development of what has been seeded during this "new moon" phase of the Saturn-Pluto cycle, through their quadrature alignment at the crossroads of a square aspect in 2028, their "full moon" opposition in 2035-2036, until they meet again in conjunction in 2053.

But in the interim, we may also turn to other planetary archetypes for meaning and guidance. Indeed, the cosmos provides us with a constant source of wisdom through the daily, weekly, monthly, and even hourly (in the case of the Moon) traversals, encounters, and relational dramas of these celestial personalities.

The Sun plods dutifully along its daily course with its closest companions, Mercury and Venus, never too far from its side, occasionally catching up ever so briefly to its slower compatriots before continuing on its steady way, and Mars blazes its trail across the sky only slightly more slowly, occasionally retracing its steps in retrograde motion spanning weeks to months before forging on ahead. Jupiter takes its sweet time, enjoying a leisurely year-long stay in each astrological sign where it can truly savor and lend its magnanimous influence to any planetary friends it might meet within each realm. Saturn gets down to business, taking a full two and a half years in each sign, including several reflective retrograde courses, in order for it to make the most of what each sign—and any compatriot planetary archetypes—have to offer, and to leave its indelible mark before taking on its next task.

But after Saturn the further planets move slowly enough to not only mark the passage of weeks and months, but years and even whole decades. Uranus, the next farthest planet to Saturn, takes a full seven years in each sign, while its neighbor, Neptune, takes twice that, and Pluto, the second most distant planetoid within the astrological pantheon, can take from 12 to 31 years, depending on the sign, due to its eccentric orbit. These "outer" planets thus leave their archetypal marks not only on the course of individual lives, but on the ethos of entire generations within the collective. Hence, when they interact with each other—and not only with the faster moving "inner" planets—they have the power to shift and define the course of humanity as a whole.

Such was the case in the 1990s, when Neptune and Uranus spent years in conjunction, along with Saturn briefly, and which saw the end of South African Apartheid simultaneously with the break-up of the USSR, the fall of the Berlin Wall, and the end of the Cold War of the previous half a century, as well as the rise of the home computer and the proliferation of the internet, both of which ushered in a new era of increased globalization and information sharing. Such was also the case in the 1960s, when Uranus and Pluto were in conjunction and which were marked by the explosion of revolutionary impulses in defiance of established power structures such as white supremacy, patriarchal chauvinism, religious dogmatism, and capitalist war-mongering.

These outer planets proceed in lengthy cycles spanning centuries—one coming into conjunction, square, or opposition with another, much as the Sun and Moon dance their monthly waltz of waxing and waning. The conjunction signals the beginning of a new cycle, the opposition its culmination, and the waxing and waning squares support in the development of the cycle's potential. Together the three dance a complicated baroque circumvolution, one swinging near as another reels far, each following their own tempo within the rhythm of a larger song.

Uranus, Neptune, and Pluto have come together in conjunction only once in recorded history, in the 6th century BCE. As Richard Tarnas discusses, these crucial decades marked a profound shift in the course of human history, with the births of many of the great religions and philosophical systems that have

246

shaped us and our world over the last two and a half millennia.[51] The next time the three came together in close aspect was in a harmonious *trine* (180°) aspect that took place in the latter half of the 18th century CE, coinciding with the height of the Western Enlightenment and the early years of the American Revolution,[52] as well as Adam Smith's writing of *The Wealth of Nations* and the subsequent birth of capitalism, all of which have been instrumental in the shaping of the modern world as we now know it.

The next closest liaison between these three outer planets will be in the mid-2020s in *sextile* (60°) and trine aspects. Pluto and Neptune have maintained a supportive sextile aspect relationship to one another since the 1940s. Pluto and Neptune together open us up to our collective shadows, for better or worse—both for the potential to heal, to find renewal and rebirth, as well as to project and play out our more sordid, shameful, unconscious, and often instinctual shadow material (Pluto) through *il*lusion or *de*lusion (Neptune). The long sextile aspect, however, offers us a collective opportunity to partake in a redemptive (Neptune) process of such shadow material through an acknowledgement and acceptance of our inherent grace and divinity, as well as of our interrelationality, in an embrace of compassionate reverence for and accountability to all beings. As Tarnas writes of this aspect between Neptune and Pluto,

> "[A] certain profound evolution of consciousness appears to be propelled and sustained in a gradual,

---

[51] *Cosmos and Psyche*, 2006, p. 409.
[52] Ibid, p. 455-456.

harmoniously unfolding manner . . . These century-long epochs generally seem to impel the collective experience of a more confluent relationship between nature and spirit, between evolutionary and instinctual forces (Pluto) and the spiritual resources and idealistic aspirations of the pervading cultural vision (Neptune)."[53]

Uranus briefly elevates this lengthy signature between Neptune and Pluto as it simultaneously forms a supportive sextile to Neptune and a harmonious trine with Pluto in 2025-2026 within the first degrees of the compatible signs of Gemini, Aries, and Aquarius, respectively.

As Tarnas states, "When it comes to the future, we are all seeing through a glass darkly,"[54] but the archetypal language of the planets can give us some glimmers, however murky, of impending themes. Pluto ingressing into Aquarius suggests a shift in emphasis to collectivity, to social organization for a common purpose, though the shadow of such might include the subjugation of individual freedoms to the social good.

Concurrently, however, Neptune ingressing into Aries indicates a period of dissolution of and perhaps a willingness to transgress the bounds of what it means to be *an individual*—we may find ourselves asking what does the "self" really mean and what is the role of the individual within such a deeply interconnected, co-dependent world? Perhaps the individual "self" can only be understood as acting within a much greater collective "Self" or "World Soul," within which the sacrality of each existent must

---

[53] *Cosmos and Psyche*, 2006, p. 482.
[54] Ibid, p. 481.

be respected and revered for its own sake for what it offers to the whole. Of course, there is also the potential for the eruption of romantic idealizations and seductive delusions about the power and role of the individual, including perhaps a retreat to a familiar idolatry of heroic celebrity, but so too there is the opportunity for a redemption of individual*ism* in a shift towards a deeper receptiveness and compassion for *all* individuals, rather than some over others.

Uranus completes the trifecta as it ingresses into Gemini, bringing a revolutionary outlook to social relationships and how we relate to one another as compatriots within our collective environment, as well as to the cultivation and exchange of radical ideas and new concepts.

Together this forthcoming signature elicits archetypal themes of cooperative relationship and the potential for a collective evolution in methods of social organization, as well as of a renegotiation of the relationship between the individual and society, and indeed between the consequences of individual*ism* and the urgently growing need for communal cooperation and solidarity. But nothing is written; it is up to us to shape the future by shaping ourselves in and through the present. How we choose to respond *now*, to this moment, will affect whatever is to come next.

If we choose to continue to deny, bury, and repress our own unconscious shadow material it will inevitably come out through the shadow facets of the planetary archetypes—nervous anxiety, rebellious antagonism, frivolous eccentricity, or fanatical idealism, in the case of Uranus; delusional fantasy, chimerical surrealism, or corrosive escapism, in the case of Neptune; and

249

tyrannical despotism, instinctive viciousness, and ruthless destruction, in the case of Pluto. But we can no longer afford such indulgences, for it is in submission to such reactionary antagonisms, soporific delusions, and primitive destructiveness that we find ourselves at this point of reckoning with our collective dying. Instead, we must muster the integrity and intentionality to call forth our better natures, to engender a new way of being human—together in this, our only world—which may sprout from the soil of radical and audacious determination, redemptive compassion and acceptance, and the courage and grace to surrender the old and familiar for the new and unknown.

If we are to build a better world, one which will sustain and respect all forms and integral diversities that make life possible on this planet, then, as the Gandhian adage says, it is incumbent upon us to "be the change we wish to see." We can use the wisdom of the astrological archetypes to guide us in such a pursuit, but we must be willing and determined to take responsibility for ourselves and choose our paths wisely. For, in the words of Antonio Machado, "we make the road by walking."

APPENDIX II

WORLD SAVINGS INITIATIVE

By William Douglas Horden

It seems inevitable that a time comes when people across the globe create a mechanism by which to exert their collective self-governance.

After all, governments have given up the pretense of serving the people they now unashamedly claim to rule. Religions fail to stand up to the state and end war by prohibiting their every adherent from any violent act. Corporations make no excuses for trading the health of people and the environment for profits. The rich keep the rest of humanity in economic bondage through market manipulation. The corporate media support the status quo, upon which their right to exist hinges.

Of course, it is a state of affairs shared by all nations. The will of the many everywhere is ignored or subverted so that governments can fulfill the will of the few. We are fast becoming a world of eight billion disaffected, dis-empowered, and disenfranchised subjects: not what we would have chosen as our common bond, perhaps—but bond it is, uniting us across borders, cultures, and ideologies.

251

Which raises the question: "What *is* the will of the many?" If we had the resources at our disposal, what would we try to accomplish? Given the instantaneous worldwide communication open to us, what can we agree on achieving? Beyond all our superficial differences, what kind of civilization do we dream of bequeathing to the coming generations? And, more specifically, what long-range problems face us all and how do we solve them?

Of course, there is a growing movement of people everywhere to effect incremental, cumulative change, such as local cooperatives, ethical sustainability, ethical treatment of animals, environmental protection, responsible consumerism, community volunteerism, and so on. These and other coordinated efforts mark our real progress as a species: our growing awareness of our collective power spreads as we find new ways to change the future through local action. But the balance of power remains stubbornly tipped in favor of the few, whose economic interests continue to trump the real-life interests of the many.

If we are to exert our collective will, we need to create our own economic resource.

The World Savings Initiative

Central concepts—
- A permanent trust is established to which everyone in the world may contribute;
- In return for their contribution, each person is entitled to vote on how the collective funds are spent;

- Regardless of how much contributed, each person receives one vote;
- No funds can be expended on projects without two-thirds approval of donors;
- An electronic forum is established whereby donors from every part of the world can advocate for specific needs to be addressed and the best ways to address them.

Peripheral points—
- A running total of donations is constantly updated on-line;
- Funds are saved and not invested, in order to avoid market manipulation;
- A yearly audit is conducted of the trust's funds;
- A donor's vote can be transferred to an heir;
- The trust is set up to accept donations of estates;
- The barest of administrative costs, to be approved by two-thirds vote of donors (these would include audit costs, paperwork for donors without computers, website administration, volunteer training, etc.).

The World Savings Initiative, then, is a truly democratic global initiative that rights the balance of power, giving the many the means to address real-world problems ignored, or created, by the few. These include, but are not limited to, large-scale projects aimed at long-range solutions affecting the wellbeing of future generations and their relationship to the natural environment.

There are, of course, numerous technical issues to be overcome in the establishment of the World Savings Initiative. Given the creative and intellectual resources of seven billion people, however, those hurdles can be cleared in good time.

Our greatest resource is our humaneness: the goodwill of people toward one another, the love of people for the land, the inventiveness of people facing common problems—these are the attributes of hearts and minds already reaching across borders and redefining humanity beyond the shattered vision of obsolete governments.

Self-governance begins somewhere. It must have the resources to enact its will.

We have the means of changing the worst of things while letting the best of things stay the same.

If not now, when? If not us, who?

MY ANARCHIST MANIFESTO[55]

By Meghan Elizabeth Tauck

I have tried so many times to write this from an objective point of view, but I can't. It would be a lie. So, I present myself a subject from within these pages. I am fallible, faulty, susceptible to all the ill whims of history, culture, and ego. I, myself, have a history from which I have found my way to this point, to this spatial and psychological moment. Everything I have ever seen and heard and experienced, everything I have ever felt, honestly, genuinely within me, has brought me to this reckoning: I am an anarchist and this is my manifesto.

I have joked that I've been an anarchist from the time I was born because my first favorite color was black. How many little white girls prefer black? We certainly aren't supposed to. But being an anarchist isn't about what you wear or liking the color black, though it is about standing in solidarity with darker, marginalized and denigrated peoples in this white supremacist world. And white or not, that's what I was, or how I felt—

---

[55] This piece was originally written in 2006 as a final paper for an undergraduate course at Harvard University. As such it reveals some of the author's both youthful idealism and, sometimes, naïve over-simplification. Nevertheless, it stands as a powerful vision for an anarchist society. The reader is encouraged to read *Living In A Time of Dying* as, in many ways, a long-awaited sequel to this piece. It has been lightly edited from the original.

marginalized and denigrated. So when someone eventually handed me a book by political prisoner Mumia Abu-Jamal[56] I got it. When Erik Marcus[57] taught me about what factory farming does to animals and the environment I got it. And when bell hooks[58] and Gary Lemons[59] finally forced me out of my privileged white world, I didn't fight to defend my ignorance because I got it. Or, at least, I started to.

From there, anarchism came naturally. At first it was a home, a sanctuary. I read Emma Goldman[60] and felt myself in her, felt her words drop like liquid fire into my belly lighting me up and turning me on. After that it became my own. I took hold and ran with it and finally things made sense.

Everything comes together in anarchy. Nothing is reduced or left out. Anarchy looks at the big picture. That is what makes anarchy fundamentally about truth and justice. And that is why I am so in love with anarchy.

~

Human life is full of paradox and confusion. We find ourselves constantly caught between seemingly opposing realities—the external, tangible, visible, living world that we can observe, study, and seek to rationally understand, and a world that we cannot see or touch, but that we can *feel* is real nonetheless. This is the realm of the internal, the metaphysical. It is the feeling-

---

[56] *Live From Death Row*. Harper Perennial, 1996.
[57] *Vegan: The New Ethics of Eating*. McBooks Press, 1998.
[58] *Teaching to Transgress*. Routledge: New York, NY, 1994.
[59] Professor, Eugene Lang College, New School University, 2001-02.
[60] *Anarchism and other essays*. Dover Publications: New York, NY, 1969.

function rather than the reasoning-function of human existence. We must have both to be truly human. As a global culture we have become too engrossed in the physical, external world and the mechanism of reason, of the mind, at the expense of the internal mechanism of the heart and the spirit. It is through the feeling-function that we love and care for and respect ourselves and one another; it is the foundation of our solidarity. And yet we have not found a way to bridge this paradox, to live in both worlds simultaneously without pitting one against the other, physical "reality" over metaphysical consciousness.

Some may call this consciousness God, Allah, Brahman, enlightenment, or "the power of the Universe," in an effort to comprehend the painful phenomenon of our inevitable physical death. What happens to us when we die? Do we go to a place called "heaven"? Are we reborn to this planet? Do we wrestle with karma? Do we choose the lives we lead? Or do we simply decay into dust? Become one with all the particles of the universe? Is there such a thing as a soul? And, if so, where does it come from and where does it go? *Why are we here?*

We struggle with this, too, not only in our inner ruminations but in our social lives as well. What is or should be the relationship between the self and society, between people with one another, between the individual and the state or collective? And as the world becomes more populous and globalized these questions become more urgent. How do we reconcile individual freedom with social responsibility? How do we live autonomously and harmoniously with all other autonomous beings?

For centuries organized religions have sought to soothe the rupture between the physical, tangible, living world, and the

257

frighteningly intangible realm of the unknown, experienced in death. Governments have sought to quell the tension between the individual and society. And both have dipped their fingers into the business of sorting out reason from morality, sense from sensibility. But these institutions fall short because they are reductive and superficial.

Though their metaphorical and mythical examples of struggle may help us to understand the circumstance of our existence, the organized, predominantly Abrahamic, religions have attempted to anthropomorphize the metaphysical, which cannot be reined in or defined in human terms. And while governments are formed to protect people from abuse or exploitation by their fellow human beings through the implementation of a system of laws, they can do so only by paternalistically disempowering their "subjects," thereby inherently undermining individual autonomy and reducing them to mere objects.

The result is that these mechanisms of social and ideological hegemony inevitably lend themselves to greater conflict and extremism—different groups fighting over whose way is more moral, whose "God" is more holy, whose system is more powerful—while the whole world goes up in flames and we are all left still questioning and still struggling.

How do we stop this downward spiral? People call for justice. But justice for whom? What does this "justice" look like? Different groups posit different conceptions of justice, some more convincing than others, and most inevitably self-serving. So how can we possibly agree?

Short answer: we can't. People are different with different cultures, different histories, different solidarities, different needs, and different talents. In fact, it is conceivable that there are infinite conceptions of what is just or unjust, as there are infinite persons in the world and throughout history.

Where does anarchy fit into this infinity? It embraces it. Because anarchy is more than simply no government. Nor is it just a synonym for chaos. Anarchy is order without oppression, community without coercion, freedom without isolation or alienation, equality without homogeneity, sustainability without exploitation. Anarchy knows no borders or laws, but it does not lack for principles or structure. Anarchy recognizes that *with great freedom comes great responsibility*.

There is no such thing as a "state of anarchy" because statehood implies stasis, occupying a static, unchanging position, and anarchy is a constant process. Its lifeblood is transformation—like a shark, if it stops moving it dies.

By the same principle there is no such thing as perfect balance, only the shifting of weights from one side to the other. There is no such thing as balance or equilibrium because life is the process of oscillating in the space between extremes. If life finds a place of balance it is only for a fleeting moment because, inevitably, as life is always moving and flowing, some element of friction presents itself, throwing off the illusion of balance and sending the subject back into weighing that space of tension.

Think of a seesaw: two people sit on either end and try to balance their weight against one another, but inevitably one of them weighs more, or their weight shifts from side to side, or a wind comes along, or one sees something out of the corner of her eye that catches her attention, she turns her head, weight is shifted and balance is lost. Or, even if they did achieve "balance," their bodies grow and shrink over time and that changes the weight differential. The point is that even if they seem to have achieved perfect balance, they are always negotiating each other's weight, the relationship between one extreme and the other. And that is a constant process. If either of them stopped this negotiation, one extreme would win over the other. Anarchy navigates this tension.

Politically, most people favor the idea of a more "balanced" social system than one that falls to any extreme. It is widely recognized, often in hindsight, that the most extremist governments throughout history are those that became the most brutal and authoritarian. Liberals and conservatives, Democrats and Republicans, constantly accuse one another of being "extremists" who are trying to shift American politics and culture to one extreme or another, whichever is in their exclusive favor. Meanwhile, those on "both" sides of the binary Left-Right American political spectrum accuse anarchists of being radical extremists. But *anarchism is radical only on a scale where oppression is the norm.*

Oppression is the act of reduction, of taking human life and rendering it down to mere bones and flesh, status and circumstance. It comes in many forms. It can be overt or covert, subtle or in-your-face. Oppression is exploitative, patronizing, violent, dehumanizing, systematic and institutionalized. Systems of oppression that operate in our current society (variably dependent on country and region) include patriarchy and sexism, white supremacy and racism (including anti-

Semitism and Islamophobia), xenophobia, classism, cisheteronormativity including homophobia and transphobia, ableism, saneism and neuronormativity, ageism and ephebiphobia (look it up), sizism and fatphobia. These oppressions have become institutionalized in our social structures, our cultures, and our minds. They reflect a dominant paradigm, the status quo; they are the social norm. What this means is that we have become so used to these oppressions being commonplace in our lives—in our positions in society and in our relationships with the people around us—that we have come to accept them, believe in them, and perpetuate them. Indeed, we have even become dependent on them and learned to revere them. We think they give our lives meaning, structure, or safety, but what they really do is separate us from ourselves and each other, divide us up into little fragments of humanity so that in the end we no longer know who we are. All we know of ourselves and each other are the arbitrary superficial signifiers we come to represent. Bones and flesh, status and circumstance.

But that cannot answer *who* we are or the purpose of our existence. Where is our substance? We feel that it is there, but where can we find it if not in the sum of our actions and experiences?

It is the reductive force that threatens us. Money and capitalism, white supremacy and racism, patriarchal sexism and cisheteronormativity, religious dogmatism, etc., are mechanisms of the reductive force that seeks to dehumanize, objectify, (ab)use, and oppress us. "These are not mere words, they are *perspectives*."[61] They are ontologies—words create worlds.

---

[61] Quote from the film "V for Vendetta," 2006.

What does it *mean* to be *de*humanized, to have your humanity stolen from you? What does it mean to be treated as an object rather than as a subject? How many forms can abuse and exploitation take? What does oppression *feel* like?

For me, it feels like *fear*—the fear of rape, fear of physical violation, fear of poverty, of not having enough to survive, fear of having my power stripped away, fear of others' indifference to my pain, or anyone else's pain, fear of abusing my power over someone else, fear of the capacity for human beings to be so inhuman(e). It feels like *sadness*—a deep, penetrating sadness, like I can feel every cut and sore and painful memory of every human being and animal and plant on this planet, and even of the planet itself. It feels like *anger*—a violent rage that wells up in me whenever I witness a transgression against the humanity or existence of another, like it is my instinctual unavoidable duty to protect them, everyone, the whole world. It feels like being trapped, powerless, incapable of living a human(e) life under inhuman(e) circumstances, in an inhuman(e) world. It feels like a death march, like a cold, calculating indifference toward life and all its complexity, depth, and subtle, simple beauty. It feels like murder, a massacre, genocide, not only of the body but of the soul and spirit (which is worse?).

I see this oppression in the school system and academia, the prison system, the courts, the America military industrial complex with its agenda of war and colonization. I see it in over two million people in prison in America, half of them Black and Latine. I see it in the death penalty, anti-abortionism, rape, hate speech and hate crimes, The Minutemen, Tea Party, Proud Boys and neo-fascists everywhere. I see it in the very existence of poverty, of homelessness, of starvation, poisoned and filthy

262

water, bottled water that you have to pay for (?!?), lack of health care, welfare, and social security, the HIV and AIDS epidemic, global warming, and over one thousand people drowned in New Orleans after Hurricane Katrina and more than twice that displaced and no one seems to give a good goddamn.[62] I see it in the histories of Gandhi, Malcolm X, Martin Luther King, Jr., Jesus, John Brown, Assata Shakur, Mumia Abu-Jamal, Leonard Peltier, Nat Turner, Frederick Douglass, Linda Brent, Sojourner Truth, Emma Goldman, Carlo Giuliani, Hiroshima, Nagasaki, the Phillipines, Puerto Rico, Indonesia, Vietnam, AFRICA, native peoples everywhere, and on and on over every inch of this planet. I see it in volatile patriotism, in the "boys will be boys" mentality, in the culture of silence around domestic violence and rape, in the indifference towards, if not active demolition of, women's rights and health. I see it in the Christian Right, the Taliban, the Israeli occupation of Palestine, and any organized religion, group, or government that uses violence and terror to exploit, exclude, or exterminate. I see it in the industries of tourism, sweatshop labor, and slavery. I see it in globalization, the IMF, WTO, and World Bank that exploit developing nations for their resources while crippling their domestic economies forcing them to become dependent on Western capitalism. I see it in Amazon, Wal-Mart, McDonalds, and every other multinational corporation that pushes small businesses *out* of business, forcing them into economic subjection. I see it in the creation of the suburbs and urban decay, in the poor, working,

---

[62] What litany of atrocities and inhumane abominations could I list in the fifteen years since this writing in 2006? The indifference to life displayed in the aftermath of Hurricane Katrina pales in comparison to that of today—the response, in many countries, to the Covid-19 pandemic alone, not to mention the immense suffering of those in Yemen, Syria, Burma/Myanmar, Bangledesh, Palestine...

middle, *and* upper classes. I see it in chemical sprays, peels, and sealants. I see it in food additives like high fructose corn syrup, dextrose, BHT, and chemical dyes like Red #40 and Yellow #5. I see it in substance abuse, eating disorders, dieting, the 9-to-die work ethic, compulsive consumerism, depression, anxiety/panic disorder, PTSD and OCD. I see this oppression in people's bodies, in the language of their movements, like they are being crushed slowly, as if from an invisible weight. I see it in people's eyes when I look at them and they look at me, like they are screaming for freedom from the inside. And I see it in myself, in my own body, in my own eyes, in my choices, my thoughts and actions, my memories, my fears, sadness, anger, and, especially, in my silences. I see it in my relationships to the people I love, and hate, and even the people I pass on the street. How do we see each other? What powers do we hold over one another? Am I afraid of you? Are you of me? Are "we" of "them"?

Where does this come from? How did we get to be this way? I know it may seem impossible to ever get to the bottom of this, to ever see it clearly, or to change it. But here is one possible explanation…

~

In the beginning there were gases and dust, and from that over billions of years this planet was created, and over still more billions of years animate life emerged. Eventually, we crawled out of the mud on the continent of Africa and began our journey to become human. In this way we are descended directly from the universe itself. Call it "God" if you will, but the point is that

264

there is a direct connection between us and something far larger, something we cannot possibly control or comprehend.

As our population grew, probably exacerbated by extreme changes in the weather (drought, flood, etc.), resources like food, water, and shelter became scarcer. Some moved away to find other territories where they could live and survive while others fought for control of resources, and history took its course.

Land was always the most precious resource, especially once our method of survival shifted from foraging to farming. But only so much land could be used by one person, family, or village, and some materials, notably food, are perishable.

Enter: currency, a system of trade using arbitrary symbols of value instead of physically necessary materials. In other words, instead of trading necessary materials directly people started placing worth on something that had no real value to sustaining the species. In some places it was gold and silver, in other places beans, or tea, or spices, but everywhere those with the most "wealth" had the most power, and vice versa. And then, probably through the threat of violence and enslavement, those with the "money" "convinced" those who had none that this "money" was of real value and that everyone had to have it in order to get the raw materials they needed to survive. This started the cycle of dependence and exploitation that continues today.

Governments were created to protect this wealth, labeling it "private property," and to determine social status and allocate honors, power, and hegemony "appropriately." Hence money and hierarchy were formed directly in relation to the existence of an institutionalized system of rule, or State. And thus government is inherently against—or indifferent to—people who have less: it is anti-poor, pro-wealth. And that is dehumanizing because it devalues organic life—people existing. This is where our social problems stem from.

Eventually some people somewhere in the world got it into their heads that their precious "money" was the be-all-end-all of human existence and thus those who had it were better than those who didn't. And so people became hell bent on collecting it, and once you collected some of it you could collect more by buying up armies to protect and pillage for you. (Think of the game Monopoly: when you get a couple of houses on Park Place and Boardwalk you know you're all set. Then you up-grade to hotels and the rest of the players don't stand a chance.) That started the cycle of greed that hasn't stopped or slowed down since. Then there was the European conquest of India, Africa, and the Americas, and there was Indigenous genocide and the slave trade, all in pursuit of land and gold. And that was the start of globalization, which has also not stopped or slowed down since.

This spawned a society based on competition, not for raw materials, but for this arbitrary signifier of wealth. Instead of growing and trading the things we needed in order to survive, we were forced to work for money—to grow food for money in order to buy food to eat; to chop wood for money to buy wood to build a house; to harvest cotton and wool and weave it into cloth in order to make money to buy a shirt, and so on and so forth. Beyond being an incredibly wasteful system, it's one that places worth on something completely superficial, arbitrary, and utterly useless rather than on the livelihood of human beings and the planet where we live.

Honestly, it totally boggles my mind how people can buy into this, how people can *not* see through this mega scam we call capitalism, money, the economy. And yet we take it for granted. We accept it. It has become the norm. We even revere and cherish it. We have been taught, indoctrinated, fooled into perpetuating our own dependence, bondage, and helotry.

People are forced to compete within this economy. We need to get a good education in order to get a good job in order to make at least enough money to purchase security for ourselves and our families in the forms of food, clothes, a house, transportation, health care, some entertainment, and, of course, future education for our children so that they, too, can get good jobs to make money to buy security, and so on and so forth for eternity.

Why do people need to compete? Because we live under a system that forces us to be either better than or worse than our neighbor, either more successful or less successful, and nobody wants to be less successful because less successful is less valued and less secure.

Of course, some people will argue that competition is natural, even fun, as in sports and games. And yes, some competition *is* natural and fun. What is *un*natural and *un*fun is when people are forced to work (and sometimes literally slave) their lives away in order to survive, or in order to prove that they are better than other people. What is unnatural and unfun is social division, isolation, and alienation, like, for example, when people are forced to fight one another for quality jobs and education. What is unnatural and unfun is being forced to compete on an unlevel playing field under the scorching heat of prejudice and systemic discrimination. And what of those who can't compete at all, be it for illness, age, or because they are differently abled? Tough? Too bad? Better luck next time?

The problem here has to do with basing judgment or worth on one's place in a hierarchy. Granted, some hierarchy is natural: people are not equal because they are different.[63] But the problem arises when hierarchy is used to dole out judgment or allocate resources. Difference should not be a justification for feelings of superiority or inferiority. If one person is better at doing one thing than another person it does not mean that they are better altogether, or that they are more worthy of praise, honor, or, indeed, survival.

And yet governments are the primary apparatus' set up to divide and subjugate people by objectifying them through the hierarchical ideologies of racism, sexism, classism, cisheteronormativity, xenophobia, and religion. Race was originally constructed to justify the systematic enslavement and murder of entire peoples in places like India, Africa, and the so-called "New World" so that they could be used to boost the economies of Europe and, later, the United States. Ever since then race has been used to justify colonialist exploitation, also known as racial capitalism, which threatens everyone's welfare by desecrating social ties and solidarities as well as the planetary ecosystem. Similarly, patriarchal cisheterosexism, national borders, and religious hegemony have been constructed to feed,

---

[63] See again my distinction between *functional* versus *subjugantional* hierarchies on page 100 of this text.

perpetuate, and reinforce the dominant capitalist status quo regime.

For government, property is the most important thing. Government is built around defining whose stuff is whose and punishing any transgression against private property. Under governments *people become property* too. Our function as "citizens" is to support the regime. We become cogs in a factory of power and hierarchy. Our bodies exist to produce and consume, upholding the economic power structure, while our minds are manipulated to perpetuate ideologies of prejudice and inequality, upholding social hierarchy. Our voices are to remain silent if not complicit. Those at the bottom of the vertical social ladder are ignored, marginalized, and, if need be, systematically abused and silenced, while those at the top are rewarded with more property, value, and power.

But *it doesn't have to be this way*. There are ways for us to live comfortably, with all the essentials and accoutrements, healthily and justly with everyone else on the planet.[64] We can all have jobs.[65] We can all have education. But racism, money,

---

[64] Update: given the current reality of climate change, which has significantly sped up since this was written in 2006, making more and more lands uninhabitable and creating inevitable food shortages, I am no longer certain that this is true, BUT it remains, and will always remain, an ideal, a fervent *hope*, worth working towards, and it does not negate, and in fact urgently affirms, that a better way of living together on this planet would be as global citizens cooperatively supporting one another and the sustainability of our collective resources.

[65] By which I mean, of course, *vocations*, a sense of purpose, personal fulfillment, and productive engagement with and contribution to the collective good, and *not* the coercive, exploitative, soul-destroying wage-slavery by which we are obligated under capitalism.

patriarchy, and religious dogmas under the safeguard of government get in the way of this possibility becoming a reality.

Governments *do not* have the power to take away the inalienable rights of *any* human being.   That's why they call them "inalienable." They're inherent, government or no.   People should not, by consent or otherwise, be ruled by any other entity but themselves and the laws of the universe, and any government or organization that assumes to preside over the rights of human beings, by *force* or otherwise, is unjust. When people give up their power to an organization or State, they give up a piece of their autonomy, their agency, and their capacity to be fully human.   They submit themselves to an external authority, thereby placing themselves on the ladder of social hierarchy and tacitly accepting and perpetuating a divisive and dehumanizing ideology of supremacy and inferiority.

And if the purpose of government is to divide, dehumanize, and define people as objects of the State according to their property and ability to produce and consume, then we need a new system. We need a system wherein necessities are shared so that everyone has what they need to live and, moreover, a system wherein value is placed on people's lives and the diversity of peoples rather than on what they have, produce, or represent.

Under such a system everyone can pursue self-actualization without surrendering respect for others in the process because people own themselves and no one else and coercion is a violation; social responsibility, i.e. compassion towards and solidarity with other people, is a higher moral incentive than self-preservation; self-preservation is less of a concern because everyone is looking out for one another; people "own" their labor and claim the fruits of their labor, and can use the resources they need to accomplish the tasks of their labor, but mutual aid and shared goods are a higher moral incentive than hoarding for one's own benefit.

Anyone who violates the ethical incentives of an individual or the community will receive help, not punishment. If a person steals because she or he needs something for their survival or self-actualization then that is an indication of the need for greater social responsibility, shared good, and mutual aid, and reflects not on the individual, but on the community as a whole. If a person steals something out of greed rather than necessity or threatens another person's life or liberty, then, depending on the substance of the crime, the context and specific details, that may indicate the need for strategic protection and/or reparations to be decided on by consensus of the community, as well as it may be an indication that she or he may need psychological and/or medical help because of either a chemical imbalance or spiritual/emotional depletion. This too reflects on the status of society, for whatever brings a person to such a state of emotional stress implicates not only the individual but the community as well. To ask what drives a person to that point and how they can be helped is a constructive response, rather than mere stigmatization and isolation. As such, all health and social services are universally available and non-stigmatized, as an obligation of mutual aid and solidarity.

But, you ask, what of human nature, the natural propensity for greed, violence, and domination? What if someone's self-actualization entails oppressing other people?

In response to this query, I ask you to look inside yourself. Are you essentially greedy and violent? And, if so, are those not the instinctual parts of you that are susceptible to the biologically ingrained fear of extinction and which answer to the fundamental evolutionary obligation for self-preservation? And yet aren't we human? Don't we have the capacity to reason and communicate, to exist together in respectful, ethical, and honorific community so long as everyone has access to what they need to survive and thrive? Isn't it, then, our duty, our human obligation, to exercise those capacities? Isn't that in favor of our evolution?

Certainly, at this point in history there are many many people who feel that their self-actualization depends on their status over other people (or under them). Those people need help, not punishment. Because beyond the basic physical necessities for the success of humanity—sustenance, security, and sex—we also need *companionship, community, love*. What happens to people who don't get that, like the so-called feral children brought up with little to no human contact? They still have the capacity to reason and to communicate with language—the two essential functions that set humans apart from animals—but they lack the exercise to do so. We need inter-human communication and support to show us how to use our human faculties. Our species would not have evolved very far if not for community. Therefore, I believe that it is *against* our nature to despise our fellow human beings, as it is against our nature to destroy our home, our place of nurturance and security, our planet Earth.

Then why do we learn to despise and destroy? One, we learn to despise because of a fear of difference—though we all descended from the same creature that crawled out of the

272

African mud we have evolved to look and speak differently and to have different customs, cultures, and religions. Probably because we were forced to compete for resources, difference—people who looked or sounded different than us—was seen as a threat to our survival. And based on those differences we came to fear and despise each other and erected social boundaries and hierarchies with the help of institutionalized systems of rule, i.e. governments.

And two, we learn to destroy because of a fear of death, of non-existence. What does it mean to not exist? If there is more to this material life—and we feel that there is—then where do we go when this life is over? We need to know, we lust to know, and yet we cannot know, and because we cannot know we hoard and fill our lives with as much material certainty and security as we can. We produce and consume. We build bigger houses, buy more cars, worry about the style of our clothes, the shape of our bodies, we define our selves by the music that we listen to, our favorite movies, the food we eat, the brands we buy, by who we choose to be our friends or by the cultures of the families we were arbitrarily born into. People even have babies as accessories, bringing more people into this world as objects to give their own lives more meaning. Our lives become the sum of our material possessions and experiences. We are bodies and minds only. We strive to live longer and know more, so that maybe, someday, we may be completely secure and fearless.

Some fixate on the elusive physical experience of happiness, euphoria. They strive for it like it is a goal to attain and enjoy forever and ever. But happiness is a temporary state, and the illusion that it can be achieved or conquered is false and leads people to spend their whole lives searching, through tangible, external, superficial means, for something that is intangible—it leads people to *do* rather than to *be*. It is my experience, and I believe, that the function of life is to be. We are here because we are here. It is our job to exist (and if I am correct then we are seriously fucking it up).

No matter what we *do* to escape the unknowable, the inevitable moment of death lurks around every corner, and so it is our fear that drives us. How ironic, since by avoiding our own demise we are not only marching straight towards global extinction, but we are objectifying ourselves into non-existence. We make a bloody career of death, from war, to poverty, to slavery, to conquest, to consumption, to global warming, to ignorance, indifference, and silence.

All this is why I am an anarchist, because I see that we have invested ourselves in our own death, and the deaths of our fellow human beings, our brothers and sisters, our parents and grandparents, our children and grandchildren. I am not trying to tug at your heartstrings or manipulate your emotions—this is not just some sentimentalist gimmick to get you to "please, think of the children." But I *am* appealing to your feeling-function, the metaphysical consciousness in all of us that tells us, shows us, that we are one. Because it is these small solidarities that teach us to love humanity as a whole. It is because we love our own families that we feel sympathy for others, that we cringe at their abuse or misfortune, and that somewhere inside we yearn to help one another: because everyone is someone's family, they might as well be (y)our family.

So, we return to the paradox of self and society, the internal and external, individual and collective, freedom and responsibility.

274

We are human. We are autonomous, thinking, feeling individuals at the same time that we *need* each other communally. We cannot escape society, but we cannot escape ourselves either. Nor can we escape life and death. As such we have an innate, inescapable responsibility to honor the freedom and consciousness and existence of every living thing on this planet.

The inescapable fact is that humanity cannot be saved. We will die out, either by an act of nature or by our own doing. But the point is not to exist eternally—each person must die, we come and we go, this has always been true. The point is to honor the *fact of our existence*, individually and collectively. It is my wish for humanity—for myself, and my sister, my brother, my parents, my lovers, and my friends, and their parents and sisters and brothers and lovers and friends—to realize this. Anarchy honors this fact. Unconditionally and uncompromisingly, anarchy loves and validates humanity, the experience of all things living on this earth.

And though we must die we must also live. I want to live. I want to live with the people I love, which, when all is said and done, is everyone, and I want to live in the place that I love and experience the earth's unending beauty and magnificence, and I want everyone that I love to live here with me, to be and be different and be always transforming and always complimenting each other's weight in a world of unending paradox. That is life and I want it until it is no longer mine, or ours, to have.

This is my anarchy. Is it yours?

ACKNOWLEDGMENTS

We are all connected. Nothing is created on its own without the support and nourishment of the community of beings and events that came before and those beings simultaneously dreamed into existence. As such we would like to offer our deepest gratitude to all of those who have supported and sustained us...

To all the medical personnel who have helped us to survive this pandemic, and stood by the deathbeds of those who did not, and to all the frontline workers who have helped to keep us fed and warm and safe throughout this time of upheaval;

To all the protesters and organizers flooding the streets and demanding justice and safety for the most vulnerable among us, especially Black, Brown, Indigenous, immigrant, and trans and nonbinary folks;

To our beloved families, teachers, and friends who have walked beside us on our respective (and collective) journeys, whose love and validation has fortified and afforded us the capacity to write these words;

And a special acknowledgment to the family of Matthew Flowers, not only for their generous permission to include the story of their beloved in these pages, but simply in honor of the vulnerable and courageous grief of their tender hearts.

Last but certainly not least, we express gratitude for the waters and soil, mycelium and insects, animals and plants with whom we share this great Earth;

For the stars and planets, with especial gratitude to the great teachers Saturn, Pluto, and Jupiter;

And for the ancestors who seeded our present with their bones and breath, and who continue to guide and support us in our travails through this living realm.

INDEX

Black people, vii, 75, 87, 92, 97-
98, 262
Black Power movement, 232
Black, Brown, Indigenous, vii,
75, 98-100, 277
blacksmith, archetype of, 34
bonding/bondage, 78, 251, 267
boundaries
emotional and physical, 104
of integrity, 107
Saturn archetype and, 235-236
between self and world, 150
social, 273
breath/breathing, 4, 123-127,
172, 180
Broadnax, Che, 97
Brunton, Paul, 196

California Institute of Integral
Studies (CIIS), 190
Capitalism, 267. *See also* white
supremacist capitalist
cisheteropatriarchy
alternative to, 173-174
birth of, 246
and colonialism/colonization,
vii, 15-16, 68
nationalism and, 52-53
neoliberal, iv, 97, 237, 241-
242
racial capitalism, 15-16, 172,
268
resistance to, 15-16, 49
chaos
as synonym for anarchy, 167,
259
climate chaos, 98, 243
social, 100
children
abused and neglected, 30-31,
92-93
advice to, 201
children's suffrage, 135

power of, 177
at waterpark, 120-122
choices
free will and, 22, 125-126, 165
hope as a choice, 49-50
making intentional, 220
cisheteropatriarchy. *See* white
supremacist capitalist
cisheteropatriarchy
civilization, modern. *See* modern
civilization
climate crisis, iv, 98, 127, 130,
243
co-creation, 22-23, 132-133, 168,
220, 234
coexistence, 112
cognitive dissonance, v, 106
Cold War, 237, 245
of psyche, 138
collective unconscious, i, 39-40
colonialism. *See also* white
supremacist capitalist
cisheteropatriarchy
colonialist exploitation, vii,
15-16, 72-73, 98-99,
220, 268
colonization, 68-72, 102, 220,
262
forces of, 130
ideology of, 70, 76
Inner Fascist and, 102-103,
166
racism and, 15-16
common good, 63
Communion
mystical, 7-8
rites of, 225
Sphere of Universal, 82
Communities
anarchy and, 167-168, 271-
272
belonging and, 82, 165
Beloved Community, 173

282

extinction
    fear of, 270-272
    mass, iv, 14, 41, 139, 171, 219
    of flora and fauna, 47
    of humanity, iii, vi, 14, 41, 60,
        219, 274

Faith/faith, 21, 132-134, 154,
        193, 213
    surrender to, 132
farming, 11, 59, 256, 265
fascism
    "all lives matter" and, 170-171
    belonging and, 78-80
    cause of, 141, 163
    defeat of, 172-173
    imperialist racial capitalism,
        172
    Inner Fascist and, 100, 103,
        140-143. *See also* Inner
        Fascist
    psychological foundation of,
        140-143
    versus socialism, 52
    Right-wing, 52-53, 100, 110,
        127-130
    white supremacist, 128
fate, 38, 125-126, 131-134, 153,
        199
fear
    control, 76
    crisis of belonging and, 79-81
    of death and aloneness, 18, 28,
        214, 223-225, 272-273
    ideology of separation and, 67,
        71-72, 81
    Inner Fascist and, 104-105,
        138-139
    instinctual, 271-272
    oppression and
        dehumanization, 262

of "others" and difference, 59,
        67, 71, 76-78, 102-104,
        272-273
Pluto and, 234
Religious Right and, 110
resistance to, 124-126
of social and ecological
        collapse, vi, 127
suffering and, 133-134, 173-
        174
trauma and, 91
veil, 215
Feeling, vii, 13, 40, 55-62, 74,
        157, 216, 253-226. *See
        also individual feelings*
anarchism and, 169, 256
avoidance of, 225
of belonging, 173
"blind emotion," 60
emotional, 78
empathy, 19, 39, 60-62
energy as God, 153-157
feeling-function, 56, 59, 61-
        62, 138, 257, 275
Flower and Song, 149
Full breadth and depth, 138
as language of psyche, 13
love, 45, 214
Pure Emotion, 7
of separation, 78
thought and action, 149
through the mirage, 208, 209
Grief and Rage, iii, 45, 219
present moment, 13
powerlessness, 234
quanta, 179-180
re-membering, 28
sensation, 44
veil, 215
Flower-and-Song, 145-151
Flowers, Matt, 192-200, 204-
        213, 216
forgetting, 109-112, 224

285

humaneness and justice. *See* justice and humaneness

human nature
  creation of, 22-23
  dark side of, 40, 93, 172
  degrading to, 91-93
  dysfunctions of, 89,143
  egoic consciousness and, 168
  harmony and, 46, 176
  nature and, 64, 85
  transformation of, 183
  understanding, 39-41, 160
human soul, 44, 89, 141–142, 236
humility, 38, 161

I Ching, 92, 149, 231
Idea/Thought, 7
identity,
  belonging and, 78-79
  Native American/indigenous, 70, 73
  self, v, 29
  wonder and manifestations, 184
Imaginal realm, 12-13
imagination, power of, 116, 177
immortality, 9, 21-22
indigeneity, 72-76
Indigenous
  animistic world views, 111
  Covid-19 pandemic, 245
  follow their lead, 72
  genocide, 16, 73, 75, 267
  Nahuatl, 224
  Taoism, 184, 188
  Tarahumara, 94
  sacred rites of communion, 225
  separate identity, 73
  women, missing and murdered, iv
  wisdom traditions, 133

individualism. *See also* separation
  alienation and, 169, 81, 143
  competition between individuals, 17
  crisis of belonging and, 70, 81
  myth/illusion of, 74, 76, 78
  redemption of, 249
  value of individual, 134
inequality, 11, 17, 41, 127-130, 237, 269
infants, 85-86, 201
inferiority. *See* superiority and inferiority
injustices, 39, 49, 129, 132, 243. *See also* justice and humaneness
Inner Fascist, 97-107, 139-143, 163-174
  belonging and, 169-170
  dichotomies and, 77
  division from self and society, 105, 138-139
  enemy-within, 138-139
  fascism and, 141
  fear and, 102-105, 138-139, 172-174
  freedom and, 107, 138-139, 165
  inner colonization, 103, 166
  joy and, 138
  as liar, 141-143
  love and, 105-106, 168
  psyche and, 101-103, 137-138, 140, 142, 172-173
  spiritual anarchy and,167-173
  superiority/inferiority and, 103, 106-107, 139-143, 164, 166, 168-170, 172, 174
  white supremacist capitalist cisheteropatriarchy and, 139-140, 170-172

287

288

self-sacrifice, 9, 21, 38
senses, viii, 7, 32-33, 132, 150, 153, 185, 214-216. *See also* perceptions
separation. *See also* individualism
  binary oppositions and, 101-102, 163
  crisis of belonging and, 67-72, 75-78, 80
  structures of, 79, 261
  experience of, 34, 78
  ideology of, 78-68, 72, 76-77, 80
  illusion of, 7, 19, 80-81, 143, 164
  the Inner Fascist and, 139
  matter and spirit, 7, 149
  as trauma, 80, 224-225
September 11, 2001, 193
service to life, 7-8, 34
shadow
  Pluto/Neptune and, 241, 247-250
  the Political Left and, 113
  of the psyche/subconscious, 98, 168, 178, 247-250
shamanism, 94
sleep, walls of, 40. *See also* dreams
Smith, Adam: *The Wealth of Nations,* 247
socialism, 52
social justice, 97, 100, 159-162, 191, 259
social realm
  balance in, 65, 160, 176, 252-253, 260
  crisis of belonging, 74-76, 78-81
  current reality in, 12, 89, 100, 172, 261
  equality in, 37, 91

evolution of, 91, 235, 249
global and inner landscapes of, 169-170
Green Society, 183-188
individual freedom vs. social good, 168, 248, 257
myths about, 74, 78, 94-95
New Contract, 159-162
social conditioning, 111
social institutions, 12, 41, 115, 159, 183, 234, 236, 258, 261
social justice, 97, 100, 159-162, 191, 259
sociopolitical structures and ideologies, 89
systems of oppression in, 141, 166, 261
uprisings in, 128, 233
solidarity
  as wisdom, 177
  belonging and, 134, 170
  community, 130, 167-168, 220, 249
  feeling-function, 257
  global, 173
  in grief, 207
  mutual aid, 272
  through anarchy, 151, 167-168, 170, 271
  with BIPOC, 255
solitude, 138
soul
  embodiment and, 46, 156
  human, 9. *See also* spirit
  nagual and, 226. *See nagual y tonal*
  soul-making, 34-38
  of World, 19, 33, 49, 61, 64, 95, 249
species-centric worldview, 64
Sphere of Universal Communion, 82

waterslide
    acceptance and surrender, 124-
        126, 132-134
    as metaphor for life and death,
        127, 131
    story of, 119-134
Whitehead, Alfred North, 48, 60,
        142, 166, 231
white supremacist capitalist
        cisheteropatriarchy
    belonging and, 75, 79
    death-cult of, 49
    dehumanization by, 140-141,
        261-262
    dis-enchantment of cosmos,
        133
    ideology of separation in, 68,
        75, 269
    indigeneity and, 75
    Inner Fascist and, 139-141,
        170, 172
    "modern" "civilization," 68,
        79
    resistance to, 49
wisdom
    astrology as source of, 245,
        250
    language of, 40
    need for, 37-38
    philosophy, 33

Spiritual Left, 112-113
    victory and, 175-178
    wisdom teachings/traditions,
        36, 64, 133, 191
women, 99
World Citizens, 94
world domination, 53
World Savings Initiative, 251–
        254
World Soul, 19, 33, 64, 95, 249
worldviews
    animistic-mystical worldview,
        34-35, 37
    belonging, based on tenets of,
        82
    Existence and Essence, 2
    materialist, 2, 35, 37
    respect for other, 73
    scarcity and fear, 81
    species-centric, 64
World War Two, 51-52
worthiness, 47, 75, 103, 139-142,
        166, 214, 267-269
wrong-doing, 29-30, 36, 39

yin-yang, 48, 147, 225. *See also*
        Taoist cosmology

Zeitgeist, 29, 242

CPSIA information can be obtained
at www.ICGtesting.com
Printed in the USA
BVHW080220300821
615259BV00004B/17